Cricket Meets AI

Transforming the Game

By
Alexis Palmer

Cricket Meets AI

Transforming the Game

Table of Contents

Introduction 1

Chapter 1: The Fusion of Cricket and AI 5

Chapter 2: Historical Perspective - From Analog to Digital 9

Chapter 3: Understanding Artificial Intelligence 13

Chapter 4: Data-Driven Player Analysis 16

Chapter 5: Enhanced Performance Metrics 20

Chapter 6: AI in Training and Practice Sessions 24

Chapter 7: Injury Prevention and Management 28
    Wearable Technology 28
    Predictive Modelling 31

Chapter 8: Smart Decision-Making 35
    On-Field Strategy 35
    Real-Time Adjustments 38

Chapter 9: Player Scouting and Recruitment 42

Chapter 10: Opponent Analysis and Strategy Formulation 46

Chapter 11: The Role of Big Data in Cricket 50

Chapter 12: AI in Umpiring and Decision Review System (DRS) 54

Chapter 13: Enhancing Fan Engagement 58
    AI-Powered Analyses 58
    Personalised Content 62

Chapter 14: Virtual and Augmented Reality...66

Chapter 15: AI in Cricket Broadcasting...70
  Commentary Enhancement..70
  Visual Analytics..74

Chapter 16: The Economic Impact of AI in Cricket.........................78

Chapter 17: Ethical Considerations in AI Usage..............................82

Chapter 18: Case Studies of AI Implementation..............................86
  Successful Examples..86
  Lessons Learned..90

Chapter 19: The Future of Training and Talent Development.........94

Chapter 20: AI's Role in Women's Cricket..98

Chapter 21: AI in Grassroots and Amateur Cricket........................102

Chapter 22: Building Smarter Stadiums...106
  Intelligent Infrastructure...106
  Fan Experience...109

Chapter 23: Real-Time Strategy Games Within Cricket..................113

Chapter 24: Global Trends and AI Adoption..................................117

Chapter 25: Voices from the Field - Insights from Experts..............121

Conclusion..126

Appendix A: Appendix..129
  Key Terms and Definitions...129
  Additional Readings..130
  Relevant Websites and Online Resources..................................130
  Academic Papers and Journals..131
  Contact and Feedback...131

Introduction

C ricket, a game deeply woven into the cultural fabric of numerous nations, has experienced unparalleled evolution over the years. What started as a leisurely pastime for English aristocrats has matured into a global phenomenon, drawing the attention of billions. From dusty village greens to iconic stadiums with colossal lighting, the sport has seamlessly blended tradition with modernity.

However, the current era heralds a revolution that is not just about the physical prowess of players or the ethereal magic of the game. We are on the cusp of a technological renaissance, where artificial intelligence (AI) is reshaping how the game is played, analysed, and even enjoyed by fans worldwide.

The integration of AI in cricket might sound like something out of a futuristic novel, but it is happening here and now. Technological advancements are not just enhancing how players train or perform, but they are also transforming every aspect of the sport. From strategy formulation to fan engagement, AI's fingerprints are everywhere.

Understanding AI's role in cricket begins with appreciating the sheer magnitude of data involved. Cricket is a game of numbers, a sport where every run, wicket, and ball can be quantified and analysed. Historically, human analysts would painstakingly pour over these statistics, seeking patterns and insights. But with AI, the analysis goes deeper, faster, and is more accurate. These algorithms can identify trends that remain invisible to the human eye.

This transformation is not just about raw data and numbers. It is about redefining the very essence of the game. Can AI help mitigate player injuries, making careers longer and more productive? Can it provide real-time insights that change the dynamics of a match? The answers to these questions prove to be inspiring chapters in cricket's unfolding narrative, powered by AI.

Consider player performance, for example. Today's cricket players are not only skilled sportsmen but also data points in a vast analytical framework. Every movement, from a bowler's arm angle to a batsman's foot placement, is studied in minute detail. AI-driven technologies enable coaches to dissect these movements, offering feedback that is both instant and invaluable.

But it's not just about player performance metrics. AI impacts the strategic dimensions of the game as well. Decision-making, a critical aspect of cricket, has been revolutionised. Leveraging AI, teams can make real-time tactical adjustments during matches. Predictive algorithms assess numerous variables, providing insights that help captains and coaches make informed decisions.

Let's not overlook injury prevention and management. Wearable technology, coupled with predictive modelling, now plays a crucial role in ensuring player fitness. These devices monitor an array of physiological parameters, and AI interprets this data to predict potential injuries before they become critical, thereby safeguarding players' health and ensuring they are at the peak of their performance.

The fan experience, too, has undergone a paradigm shift. Modern-day fans demand more than just watching the game. They seek immersive experiences, real-time data, and personalised content. Enter AI, with its ability to deliver tailor-made experiences to fans based on their preferences, making every match feel uniquely personal.

In the age of digital engagement, AI also powers analytical tools that break down complex game strategies and performances into digestible snippets. Fans are no longer passive spectators; they become active participants in the narrative of the game. Detailed graphics and insightful commentaries bring them closer to the action than ever before.

Certainly, the integration of AI in cricket has a profound economic impact. Teams, broadcasters, and even sponsors are leveraging AI to optimise their investments. Intelligent algorithms predict match outcomes and player performances, aiding in decision-making processes that range from team selections to marketing strategies.

Nevertheless, with great power comes great responsibility. The ethical considerations surrounding AI usage can't be ignored. From data privacy to fairness in algorithmic decision-making, there is a need for a balanced approach that safeguards the essence of the sport. Ethical frameworks must evolve in tandem with technological advancements to ensure AI's application in cricket remains just and transparent.

Imagine what the future holds in terms of training and talent development. Could AI be the differentiator that helps uncover the next cricketing prodigy from the grassroots level? Could it democratise access to high-quality coaching, extending its reach to the remotest corners of cricket-loving nations? The potential is staggering and lends an optimistic outlook to the evolving landscape of cricket.

While AI's current applications are already impressive, its future potential is limitless. Virtual and augmented reality technologies are set to redefine training sessions and fan experiences alike. AI could make the cricket stadiums of tomorrow smarter and more interactive, creating an environment that is as dynamic as the game itself.

Ultimately, this book is a journey through this fascinating intersection of cricket and artificial intelligence. Whether you are a cricket enthusiast, a sports analyst, or a tech-savvy reader, the chapters ahead will illuminate how AI is not just revolutionising a sport but is creating a symbiotic relationship where technology and tradition coexist harmoniously, each enhancing the other.

So, as we embark on this exploration, let's appreciate the game of cricket in its new avatar. This is not just about technology infiltrating sport; it is a renaissance – a new beginning where cricket becomes a testament to the endless possibilities of human ingenuity and technological prowess.

Chapter 1:
The Fusion of Cricket and AI

As the pitch lights up and the stands buzz with anticipation, a silent revolution unfolds in the background. Cricket, a sport deeply rooted in tradition and history, is on the brink of a technological renaissance. The honeyed voice of the commentator may still be the same, as are the green fields and the white kits, but beneath the surface, something profound is changing. The game is evolving, driven by the intricate dance of artificial intelligence (AI) and cutting-edge technology.

AI, once a distant concept relegated to the realms of science fiction and futuristic visions, is now making tangible waves in the cricket world. It's not merely about robots or automated systems; it's about leveraging vast amounts of data to make smarter decisions, enhancing player performance, and, ultimately, changing how the game is played and consumed. The evolution is subtle yet impactful, weaving into the very fabric of the sport.

The story of cricket and AI is not just about technical advancements but also about a new symbiosis that enriches the sport for all stakeholders. For players, it means more personalised training regimens and recovery plans. For coaches, it's about making more informed strategic decisions. For fans, it means a richer, more engaging experience. Everyone stands to gain as AI permeates through the layers of the sport.

Imagine a scenario where a batsman walks onto the field, not just armed with skill and practice but equipped with insights derived from hours of AI analysis. Every bowl, every angle, every fielder's position has been studied and deconstructed. The batsman knows not just what to expect but what to anticipate. This is not a futuristic fantasy but a growing reality, one that bridges the gap between human intuition and machine precision.

The journey of integrating AI into cricket begins with data. Every match, every delivery, every stroke contributes to an extensive database. AI systems process this information, uncovering patterns and trends that might elude even the most seasoned cricketing minds. This treasure trove of data serves as the backbone for predictive analytics, helping teams strategise with unprecedented accuracy.

Take, for instance, the bowler's conundrum. Traditionally, a bowler relies on intuition, experience, and perhaps a nod from the captain to decide on the next delivery. But with AI, the decision-making process becomes far more nuanced. Machine learning algorithms analyse years of performance data, studying the batsman's weaknesses, the pitch conditions, and even the weather patterns. The result? A bowling strategy that's as much a product of scientific precision as it is of pure skill.

This fusion of cricket and AI doesn't end with players and coaches. The impact extends to the die-hard fans and casual viewers alike. Advanced AI-powered analytics offer new layers of game insights, from heat maps showing a batsman's favourite shots to predictive models that forecast match outcomes. Such innovations cater to the modern fan's desire for deeper engagement and understanding, transcending traditional boundaries and redefining how we experience cricket.

Even the way matches are broadcast is undergoing a transformation. AI-driven visual analytics and live commentary enhancements add a dynamic, real-time element to the viewing experience. One can receive instant, detailed analyses of a batsman's form, a bowler's performance pattern, or even the effectiveness of field placements—all on the fly. This isn't just about adding sparkle to broadcasts; it's about creating a more informed, immersive experience for every spectator.

However, it's crucial to acknowledge that such a pivotal transformation doesn't come without its challenges. Integrating AI into cricket necessitates a range of technical, ethical, and practical considerations. Data accuracy and integrity become paramount, as flawed data can lead to misleading outcomes. Moreover, there's the ever-present debate about the role of human intuition versus machine-driven decisions. Finding a harmonious balance between the two is both the challenge and the goal.

But hurdles aside, the potential benefits of this fusion are staggering. Imagine a world where AI helps prevent injuries by predicting a player's physical limits or identifying early signs of strain. Or a setting where budding talent can be unearthed through sophisticated AI scouting systems. These possibilities are not just exciting; they're transformative, heralding a future where cricket and AI coexist to elevate the sport to new heights.

It's also worth noting the global implications. AI in cricket isn't confined to a handful of elite teams or leagues. As technology becomes more accessible, its benefits can trickle down to grassroots levels, offering even amateur players a taste of professional-grade insights and training methods. This democratisation of technology ensures that the sport grows holistically, nurturing talent at every level and in every corner of the globe.

The fusion of cricket and AI isn't a fleeting trend; it's the future. As we stand at the cusp of this technological evolution, the possibilities are as vast as they are thrilling. AI's role in cricket is set to expand, continually pushing the boundaries of what's possible and redefining our understanding and appreciation of the game.

In this brave new world, cricket retains its timeless charm and human spirit while embracing the capabilities of modern technology. It's this harmonious blend of tradition and innovation that promises a richer, more compelling future for the sport. Whether you're a player, a coach, or a fan, the fusion of cricket and AI offers a new lens through which to view the beautiful game, making it not just a sport but a fascinating confluence of skill, data, and limitless potential.

Chapter 2:
Historical Perspective -
From Analog to Digital

The shift from analog to digital in the world of cricket has been nothing short of revolutionary. Traditional methods that relied heavily on human judgement and skill have gradually made way for sophisticated digital technologies and artificial intelligence (AI). This transformation has not only enhanced the accuracy and efficiency of the game but also reshaped strategies, training, and fan experiences.

In the days when cricket was primarily an analog sport, data collection was a painstakingly manual process. Scorers documented every ball, run, and wicket by hand, and these records formed the backbone for player statistics and game analysis. The tools were simple: scorebooks, paper, pencils, and an astute eye for detail. This analog approach had its limitations, often resulting in human errors and delayed access to critical information.

Gradually, technology started to seep into cricket. One of the earliest steps towards digitalisation was the use of video recording. Coaches and players saw the value in reviewing match footage to identify areas of improvement. Slow-motion replays became a staple in analysing critical moments of the game—whether it was a controversial dismissal or a vital technique adjustment. Still, the process was cumbersome, and the data extracted was minimal compared to today's standards.

The advent of personal computers more widely available in the 80s and 90s brought an essential shift. Software solutions began to emerge, enabling more sophisticated record-keeping and analysis. Cricket analysts started using spreadsheets and early database systems to store and manipulate data. This era laid the groundwork for more complex data analytics by offering structured, accessible data. Yet, it remained at the early stages of what we now understand as digital transformation.

The late 1990s and early 2000s marked the beginning of a significant technological boom. Internet penetration and advancements in mobile technology changed the landscape dramatically. Cricket boards and organisations began digitising historical records, making them accessible online. Fans and analysts could now engage with the data more interactively, creating a more informed and engaged cricketing community. Websites dedicated to match statistics and player profiles began to flourish, bringing a data-rich dimension to how cricket was consumed and analysed.

At the same time, innovations in broadcasting brought digital enhancements directly to the audience's living rooms. Hawk-Eye technology, initially used in tennis, was adapted for cricket to track ball trajectories. This offered unprecedented accuracy in determining LBW (Leg Before Wicket) decisions and enhanced the viewer's experience. The Decision Review System (DRS) followed, integrating technologies like Hawk-Eye, Hotspot, and Snickometer to make umpiring decisions more accurate and transparent.

As we segued into the 2010s, the concept of Big Data started making waves across various industries, including sports. Baseball had already set a precedent with sabermetrics, but cricket was quick to catch up. The increasing availability of granular data—every ball bowled, every shot played, every fielder's position logged—enabled analysts to derive insights that were previously unimaginable. This data explosion resulted in more detailed performance metrics, aiding teams in fine-tuning strategies and optimising player performance.

The integration of AI took this digital revolution to a new level. AI algorithms can process massive datasets far quicker and more accurately than any human could. Machine learning models have been trained to predict match outcomes, player performances, and even identify potential injury risks. These technologies are not just enhancing the current state of cricket; they're redefining its future.

The implications are vast. For instance, AI-driven data analytics can dissect a bowler's technique down to minute details, offering personalised training programs. Coaches can use this data to make real-time adjustments to game strategies, giving their teams a competitive edge. AI's predictive capabilities can identify emerging talents by analysing performance trends over time, making the recruitment process more efficient.

Fan engagement has also been vastly improved through digital means. Social media platforms, equipped with AI algorithms, offer personalised content to fans, keeping them more engaged and connected to their favourite teams and players. Digital platforms provide real-time statistics and interactive features that enrich the viewing experience, making every match not just a spectacle but an analytic exhibition.

Moreover, AI and digitalisation have democratized cricket. Smaller teams and less affluent cricket boards now have access to tools that were once the preserve of the elite. This levelling of the playing field ensures that talent, rather than resources, becomes the determining factor in a team's success. Emerging players from grassroots levels can be identified and nurtured in ways that were once considered implausible.

Historically, cricket has been a sport steeped in tradition, but it's also shown a remarkable ability to adapt and integrate new technologies. From early analog methods to the digital behemoths of today, the journey has been one of relentless innovation. The transition wasn't without its skeptics, but the undeniable benefits have silenced many critics. Today, the fusion of analog and digital techniques continues to propel the sport into a new era, one where data and intuition work hand in hand.

The transformation from analog to digital in cricket serves as a testament to the sport's resilience and adaptability. What began as a cautious embrace of technology has blossomed into an integral aspect of the game. As digital solutions become even more advanced, and as AI continues to evolve, cricket will undoubtedly continue to pioneer new ways to enhance performance, engage fans, and push the boundaries of what's possible on and off the field.

Chapter 3:
Understanding Artificial Intelligence

Artificial Intelligence (AI) isn't just a catchphrase; it encompasses a robust range of technologies and techniques that simulate human intelligence processes. When applied to cricket, AI serves as a transformative bedrock that can revolutionise how players train, strategise, and perform.

At its core, AI revolves around the ability to learn from data, identify patterns, and make decisions with minimal human intervention. Historically confined to science fiction, the concept has now permeated various industries, from healthcare to finance. And now, it's making waves in the world of cricket.

Machine Learning (ML) is a critical subset of AI, and it's pivotal in understanding the immense data involved in cricket. ML algorithms analyse massive datasets, extracting meaningful insights which were previously unattainable with traditional methods. These insights can help predict player performance, tailor training programs, and devise game strategies. For instance, by analysing past matches, ML can forecast the probable outcomes of future games or even a specific delivery.

Natural Language Processing (NLP) is another fascinating facet of AI. This technology enables machines to understand and respond in human language. In cricket, NLP can sift through umpteen archives of text commentary, match reports, and player interviews to extract actionable intelligence. By doing so, it provides teams with additional layers of analysis, enhancing their strategic planning.

However, AI isn't a monolithic entity but a collection of technologies that also include neural networks and deep learning. These systems are designed to recognise complex patterns and correlations that would be invisible to the naked eye. In cricket, this means AI can decipher a batsman's tendencies, bowlers' strategies, and even the psychological dimensions of players—all by analysing video footage and statistical data.

In practice, AI serves as an extension of the human analyst. While human expertise remains invaluable, AI offers a level of depth, speed, and precision that is unprecedented. This synergy can elevate not just individual performances but redefine team dynamics altogether.

One of the fundamental aspects of AI is its ability to adapt and improve over time. Unlike static algorithms, machine learning models continually refine themselves based on the new data they ingest. In cricket, this means a batting coach could have an adaptive training module that evolves with every session, consistently introducing new drills designed to address the player's weaknesses while reinforcing their strengths.

For those sceptical about AI, it's important to stress that AI doesn't replace human intuition and expertise; it augments them. Cricket is a game of uncertainties where no amount of data can predict outcomes with 100% accuracy. Nevertheless, AI can provide a competitive edge by delivering insights grounded in vast datasets, thus enabling more informed decision-making.

Applications of AI in cricket aren't limited to on-field performances alone. Off the field, AI excels in enhancing fan engagement, providing real-time analysis, and offering personalised content. By understanding audience preferences through data analytics, AI can curate a more engaging and interactive viewer experience.

Furthermore, AI techniques also find applications in injury prediction and management, an area of paramount importance in cricket. By closely monitoring players' physical parameters and workload, AI can predict the likelihood of injuries, allowing timely intervention and treatment. This not only extends players' careers but also ensures they remain in peak physical condition throughout.

The use of AI in cricket isn't a fleeting trend; it's a paradigm shift that will redefine the sport's future. From grassroots development to elite performance, AI's influence will permeate every level of the game. As algorithms become more sophisticated, the predictive power and accuracy of AI models will only improve, making them indispensable tools for teams and coaches.

Yet, understanding AI also entails recognising its limitations and ethical considerations. Questions around data privacy, the potential for misuse, and the need for transparency are critical aspects that must be addressed. Ethical AI is not just a buzzword but a necessity to ensure that the benefits of these technologies are enjoyed while minimising potential harms.

To summarise, understanding AI is about more than just grasping its technical intricacies. It involves appreciating its potential to overhaul traditional practices, its limitations, and the ethical considerations surrounding its use. As AI continues to evolve, so too will the landscape of cricket, making it an even more thrilling and dynamic sport. Whether you're on the field or off it, the integration of AI promises to be a game-changer.

In upcoming chapters, we will delve deeper into specific roles AI plays in various facets of cricket, offering a clearer view of how this technology is woven into the very fabric of the game. This includes exploring data-driven player analysis, enhanced performance metrics, and AI's role in training sessions. So, stay intrigued as we embark on this enlightening journey into the future of cricket.

Chapter 4:
Data-Driven Player Analysis

In modern cricket, the margin between winning and losing can often be razor-thin. One of the critical aspects that can tip the scales is data-driven player analysis. The advent of artificial intelligence has introduced an unprecedented level of granularity in examining players' performances, enabling teams to make informed decisions that are anchored in meticulous statistical insights. This chapter explores how AI leverages data to transform traditional player analysis into a robust, precise science.

At the core is the collection of various metrics through advanced sensors and video analysis. Every aspect of a player's performance, from the nuances of their batting stance to the exact speed and spin of their deliveries, is meticulously documented. This trove of data is then funnelled into sophisticated AI algorithms capable of identifying patterns that would be impossible for a human analyst to discern. This synthesis of detailed data points forms the bedrock of a more nuanced and in-depth player analysis.

Better understanding a player's strengths and weaknesses helps coaches tailor training programs to individual needs. It's no longer sufficient to know a bowler's average speed; AI can reveal the precise conditions under which a bowler is most effective, be it the type of pitch, weather conditions, or the phase of the game. Similarly, for batsmen, AI can differentiate how a player performs against different types of bowlers, providing an all-encompassing view that can be strategised upon for maximum efficiency.

The analysis extends beyond individual capabilities. AI delves into aspects such as player fatigue, mental resilience, and adaptability under pressure. By reviewing historical data, AI can predict when a player is likely to be performing below their optimum, thereby advising on necessary rest periods or targeted mental conditioning. This level of personalisation resonates with players and coaches alike, who can both see tangible improvements, tailored explicitly for them through these analyses.

Real-time performance tracking is another frontier where AI is making significant strides. In practice sessions or live matches, AI systems can immediately process and interpret data, offering instant feedback. This immediacy allows for rapid adjustments, be it in a batsman's technique or a bowler's delivery style. As a result, mistakes can be rectified on the fly, offering a dynamic approach to ongoing player development.

Additionally, AI has the knack for historical comparison, thereby offering a lens to evaluate contemporary players against legends of the past. By establishing performance baselines and benchmarks, AI provides a relative gauge of a player's standing, which is invaluable for team selection, role assignment, and even contract negotiations. Statistical tools such as simulated projections can estimate a player's future performance trajectory, impacting long-term strategic planning for teams and boards.

Another key aspect involves injury management. AI aids in identifying markers that indicate susceptibility to injuries. By analysing a player's biomechanical data, AI can recognize stress points and recommend modifications to techniques or training intensity to prevent injuries before they occur. Thus, it takes the guesswork out of injury prevention, contributing to a player's longevity and sustained performance.

Analysing opponents is also a critical part of the equation. Just as teams use AI to assess their players, they can dissect an opponent's game to exploit potential weaknesses. Through comparative data analysis, AI can suggest potential strategies tailored specifically to the abilities of different players, making it possible to micro-manage tactics at a level previously unimaginable. Whether it's a specific length to bowl to a batsman or a field placement that historically incurs mistakes, these data-driven insights offer a significant competitive edge.

Incorporating AI-driven data analysis into cricket raises many pertinent questions about the traditional ethos of the game. Purists may argue that an over-reliance on data could undermine the 'human element' inherent to cricket. However, proponents contend that AI serves to enhance human decision-making rather than replace it. Coaches still possess the final call, armed with actionable intelligence generated by AI, thus striking a balance between instinct and information.

Teams can now create player profiles enriched with layers of statistics, performance trends, and predictive analytics that go beyond what the naked eye can observe. Not only does this revolutionise talent scouting and team formation, but it also democratises cricket expertise, giving smaller teams access to the same level of detailed analysis that well-funded cricket boards enjoy. This levelling of the playing field holds significant implications for the sport's global landscape.

For all its advantages, data-driven player analysis also invites ethical considerations. The extent to which player data should be utilised, stored, and shared comes under scrutiny. Concerns about privacy and data security necessitate stringent governance policies, ensuring that the wealth of information gathered serves the player's and team's best interests without infringing on personal liberties. Transparency in data usage policies will be essential in maintaining trust among players, teams, and fans alike.

In summary, the realm of player analysis has undergone a seismic shift, largely driven by the capabilities of AI. Through detailed metrics, real-time feedback, injury prevention, and opponent analysis, the depth and precision offered by data-driven strategies have redefined the paradigms of player development and strategic planning. As technology continues to evolve, its role in cricket is set to become even more ingrained, promising a future where decisions are informed by the rigorous dissection of data, coupled with the irreplaceable instinct of seasoned professionals.

Ultimately, AI offers a path to excellence, one where the full potential of both current and upcoming cricketers can be harnessed and realised. The implications of such advancements are profound, touching every aspect of the sport and pushing the boundaries of what is possible. Embracing this technological revolution can propel cricket into a new era, one characterised by enhanced performance, strategic brilliance, and an unyielding pursuit of excellence.

Chapter 5:
Enhanced Performance Metrics

When discussing enhanced performance metrics in cricket, we're diving into what differentiates good players from great ones. Traditional statistics like runs scored, wickets taken, batting averages, and bowling averages provide a broad understanding of a player's ability. However, artificial intelligence (AI) allows us to dig deeper, reaching levels of precision previously unimaginable.

Let's consider a classic example—Sachin Tendulkar. Historically, his greatness was measured by his sheer number of runs and centuries. But what if we could measure his impact in specific game contexts or his adaptability to different types of bowlers? Enhanced performance metrics, powered by AI, make this possible. By analysing ball-by-ball data, video footage, and situational contexts, AI can assess how a player like Tendulkar adapted his batting style to different bowlers, pitches, and match situations.

So, what exactly are "enhanced performance metrics"? These are refined, highly specific data points that reveal detailed insights into player performances. Traditional metrics are often aggregates; they summarise larger trends but miss the micro-level details. Enhanced metrics, on the other hand, capture the nuances. They answer questions like, "How does a batsman perform under pressure?", "How effective is a bowler in the death overs?", or "Which fielding setups minimise runs effectively?"

Imagine a bowler like Shane Warne. Traditional stats highlight his impressive wicket tally and bowling average. Enhanced metrics delve deeper, revealing his success rate against left-handed vs. right-handed batsmen, his effectiveness with different variations of spin, and even the psychological impact of his sledging on opposing batsmen. AI algorithms analyse this wealth of data to produce intricate and actionable insights that go beyond mere numbers on a scorecard.

Let's break down how AI enhances these performance metrics. Firstly, there's the enormous volume of data collected from modern cricket matches. Advanced sensors, HD video cameras, and ball-tracking technologies like Hawk-Eye provide granular data points. AI processes this data to extract insights. Machine learning models identify patterns, distinguish anomalies, and predict future performance trends based on historical data.

Consider predicting a batsman's propensity to be dismissed by a particular type of delivery. It's not just about the balls he's faced from that bowler but also his footwork, shot selection, and even his body language. AI analyses thousands of data points to predict vulnerabilities. This intelligence becomes immensely useful for coaches and analysts, impacting training sessions and match preparations.

One of the groundbreaking advancements facilitated by AI is real-time performance analytics. Gone are the days when analytical insights were only accessible post-match. Today, AI equips teams with real-time data during matches. Coaches and analysts can provide instantaneous feedback, making tactical adjustments on the fly. For example, if a spinner's wrist position is detected to be inconsistent, the coach can address this immediately rather than waiting until the end of the day.

Descending deeper into the bowels of precision, we unearth another intriguing application: cognitive and emotional analytics. These metrics analyze a player's mental state—an aspect equally critical to performance. By evaluating micro-expressions, body language, and eye movement during high-pressure situations, AI algorithms gauge confidence levels, stress, and concentration. This offers an unprecedented understanding of a player's psychological resilience, invaluable for mental conditioning and strategic planning.

AI also assists in understanding the "impact value" of individual performances. Traditional metrics might record two players each scoring a fifty, but enhanced metrics distinguish the impact of those fifties based on match context. Was it scored under difficult pitch conditions? Did it come at a critical juncture in a high-pressure chase? Enhanced performance metrics provide these insights, offering a richer, contextually nuanced understanding of the game.

In dynamic sports like cricket, adaptability is crucial. Enhanced performance metrics facilitated by AI provide a detailed analysis of how players adapt to different conditions. From pitch conditions to varying levels of opposition strength, AI can track and predict a player's performance against an array of variables. This adaptability index could become a key component in future player evaluations, aiding selectors and coaches in decision-making processes.

Fielding is another area that benefits significantly from enhanced metrics. Traditional fielding stats often highlight catches and run-outs but overlook ground covered, reaction times, and positioning efficiency. AI integrates data from multiple angles and situations, presenting a complete picture of a fielder's effectiveness. It helps identify weaknesses in positioning, allowing teams to optimize field settings strategically.

Moreover, AI-driven metrics give an edge in injury management. By analyzing players' biomechanics and physical exertion, AI can predict injury risks and suggest preventive strategies. Wearable technology monitors players' movements, and AI algorithms identify stress points and fatigue levels. This proactive approach not only enhances performance but also extends players' careers by minimizing injury risks.

While enhanced performance metrics provide numerous advantages, they also raise ethical questions. Data privacy, the psychological impact of constant monitoring, and the potential for data manipulation are concerns that need addressing. It's essential to balance AI's benefits with ethical considerations to protect players' rights and well-being while fostering a sportive culture.

In conclusion, the fusion of AI with cricket has revolutionised performance metrics, providing granular, real-time, and contextually rich insights. Enhanced metrics are reshaping how we understand and evaluate player performances, offering a multi-dimensional view of the game. With AI's continual evolution, the future holds even more sophisticated metrics, pushing the boundaries of cricket analysis and enriching the sport for players, coaches, analysts, and fans alike.

The next chapter explores how these advanced metrics transform training and practice sessions, enhancing skills and strategies to elevate the game to unprecedented levels.

Chapter 6:
AI in Training and Practice Sessions

As we step into the realm of artificial intelligence in cricket, the impact it has on training and practice sessions is nothing short of transformative. Gone are the days when practice sessions were solely based on intuition, experience, and the watchful eyes of coaches. Now, AI brings an unprecedented level of objectivity, precision, and enrichment to player development.

The integration of AI in training sessions begins with data collection. High-speed cameras, sensors, and wearables gather an immense wealth of information about every move a player makes. These devices track everything from a bowler's arm speed to a batsman's footwork. The plethora of data collected allows AI algorithms to generate insights that would be nearly impossible to discern with the naked eye.

One of the most captivating advancements is the use of computer vision and machine learning to analyse a player's biomechanics. By processing video footage, these technologies can break down complex movements into fine details. This analysis provides precise metrics on angles, forces, and velocities involved in a player's actions. Coaches can then use this information to make data-driven decisions to refine techniques, enhance performance, and reduce injury risks.

Additionally, AI-driven simulations offer players realistic and immersive practice environments. Virtual reality (VR) training systems enable players to face bowlers and fielders in a controlled yet realistic setting. These systems provide a variety of scenarios, from facing a fast bowler in a high-pressure situation to practicing against a tricky spinner on a turning pitch. Such simulations allow players to hone their skills and adjust their strategies without the physical and logistical constraints of traditional practice sessions.

Let us not forget the role of predictive analytics in training. By analysing historical performance data, AI can foresee potential areas of improvement for each individual player. For instance, if a batsman often struggles with deliveries coming in at a certain angle, these insights can be used to tailor specific practice drills to address this weakness. Customisation of training regimes ensures each player maximises their potential by focusing on their unique needs.

AI also leverages natural language processing (NLP) to provide real-time feedback. Voice-activated assistants integrated into practice equipment can offer instant insights and suggestions. For example, a virtual coach might tell a bowler to adjust their wrist position to achieve a better swing. This immediate feedback loop accelerates the learning process and helps players make swift adjustments on the fly.

Let's delve deeper into how AI enhances team practice sessions. When training as a collective group, it's crucial to simulate real-match conditions. AI-powered analytical tools can reconstruct the gameplay and tactics of upcoming opponents through detailed video analysis. This allows teams to practice specific strategies and scenarios they are likely to face. Such meticulous preparation greatly increases the chances of success on the field.

Furthermore, AI systems can identify patterns in team dynamics and interactions. By tracking player movements and decision-making during practice, AI can determine the efficacy of certain formations and strategies. Insights gleaned from this analysis help in fine-tuning team cohesion and game plans, ensuring that each player understands their role and the optimal way to execute it.

Let's not overlook the psychological aspect of training. AI-based mental conditioning tools analyse cognitive and emotional responses during practice sessions. Tools such as biofeedback sensors monitor stress levels, focus, and emotional states. These insights guide psychological training, helping players develop mental resilience, focus, and the ability to stay calm under pressure. The role of AI thus extends beyond physical performance, shaping the mental framework essential for high-stakes competition.

Innovation continues with AI-driven fitness and conditioning programmes. Traditional fitness regimes often adopt a one-size-fits-all approach. In contrast, AI customises these programmes based on individual physiological data. Wearable devices track parameters like heart rate variability, sleep patterns, and energy expenditure. This data enables AI to curate fitness plans that consider each player's unique needs and recovery times, thus promoting optimal physical conditioning.

AI isn't just about improvement; it's also about innovation. One groundbreaking development is the use of AI to create hyper-personalised training plans. By understanding each player's strengths and weaknesses at an intricate level, AI can design practice sessions that not only target areas of improvement but also bolster inherent strengths. This dual focus ensures a holistic enhancement of performance.

Another significant advantage comes in the form of data democratisation. AI platforms provide access to manifold insights easily. Players and coaches can tap into a shared database filled with performance metrics, historical data, and predictive outcomes. This information is crucial for creating informed strategies and nuanced training programmes.

Yet, with technology comes the challenge of adaptation. Traditional setups might resist AI integration due to a learning curve or fear of obsolescence. However, combining AI's precision with human expertise creates an unbeatable synergy. Coaches' roles morph from simply instructing to interpreting AI-driven data and delivering it in a context players can relate to. This collaborative approach ensures that the human element in training remains invaluable.

As AI continues to evolve, so does its capacity to provide actionable insights. The future of cricket training looks more predictive and prescriptive, with AI providing real-time adjustments during practice sessions. Imagine a smart practice net that adjusts its difficulty based on the player's performance, or a ball machine programmed to deliver spins and speeds mimicking real match conditions. These advancements not only make practices more effective but also more engaging.

In conclusion, AI is revolutionising training and practice sessions in cricket. With its ability to analyse immense quantities of data, provide real-time feedback, simulate environments, and tailor fitness plans, AI enhances every aspect of a player's development. It is not just about correcting flaws; it is about unlocking a player's full potential, making training sessions more scientific, efficient, and effective. As we embrace these technologies, the future of cricket looks brighter, with players more prepared and equipped to excel in every facet of the game.

Chapter 7:
Injury Prevention and Management

In the high-stakes world of cricket, where every run and wicket can tip the scales, the importance of injury prevention and management cannot be overstated. AI-driven technologies have stepped onto the field as game-changers, offering sophisticated methods to keep players at their peak. By harnessing wearable technology and predictive modelling, teams can now anticipate potential injuries before they happen, allowing for preemptive action and tailored training routines to mitigate risks. This intelligent approach not only prolongs careers but also maintains team performance levels across seasons. As AI continues to evolve, it presents a compelling promise—not just of advancing athletic prowess but of safeguarding the very athletes who give the sport its lifeblood.

Wearable Technology

Wearable technology in cricket is not just a trend; it's a game-changer that merges the worlds of sports and artificial intelligence like never before. These devices, ranging from advanced smartwatches to state-of-the-art sensor-equipped clothing, are revolutionising both injury prevention and management in cricket. By providing real-time data and personalised feedback, wearable technology ensures that players stay in peak condition and mitigate the risks of injuries.

One of the primary benefits of wearable technology is its ability to monitor physiological metrics continuously. Devices can track heart rate, body temperature, and hydration levels, offering insights that were previously unattainable without invasive methods. For instance, a rise in body temperature or an elevated heart rate can indicate fatigue or over-exertion, providing a timely opportunity to intervene before an injury occurs. This sort of granular data empowers coaches and medical staff to make informed decisions, thus optimising training sessions and match performances.

In cricket, workload management is crucial, especially given the sport's demanding schedule. Wearable devices can measure the intensity and volume of physical activities, ensuring players do not exceed their physical limits. Fast bowlers, for example, undergo enormous strain on their shoulders and backs. Wearable sensors can track the biomechanical loads experienced by these players, enabling tailored recovery programmes that minimise the risk of stress fractures and muscle injuries.

Moreover, wearable technology is key in tracking recovery and rehabilitation. Post-injury, athletes often go through rigorous rehabilitation programmes that require precise monitoring to gauge progress. Devices integrated with AI algorithms can provide real-time updates on a player's recovery status, making it easier to assess whether they are ready to return to play. This reduces the likelihood of re-injury and ensures a safer, more effective return to the sport. The combination of wearable tech and AI helps in creating customised rehab plans that adapt to the individual's progress, thus minimising downtime and maximising recovery efficiency.

The psychological aspect of injury management shouldn't be overlooked either. Wearables can help in monitoring mental fatigue and stress levels. Cricketers often face immense pressure, and mental stress can manifest physically, leading to injuries. By analysing metrics related to stress and fatigue, wearables offer a holistic view of a player's well-being, allowing for interventions that address not only physical but also mental health.

Beyond individual benefits, wearable technology also plays a significant role in team dynamics. Data collected from each player contributes to a comprehensive dataset that coaches can use to adapt training programs for the entire team. Patterns and trends highlighted by this data can reveal underlying issues that may lead to injuries. For example, if multiple players are showing signs of fatigue, it may indicate that the training intensity needs to be reduced or altered. This proactive approach helps in maintaining optimal team performance while reducing injury risks.

Injury prevention is not just about addressing current issues; it's also about predicting future ones. Predictive analytics powered by AI algorithms embedded in wearables can forecast potential injuries based on current and historical data. These predictions allow preemptive measures to be taken, such as adjusting a player's workload or providing targeted physiotherapy to vulnerable areas. This foresight can be a game-changer in professional cricket, where preventing an injury can make the difference between winning and losing a series.

However, the success of wearable technology in injury prevention and management hinges on the seamless integration of these devices into the existing sporting infrastructure. Cricket teams and medical staff must be trained to interpret the data accurately and respond effectively. There needs to be a collaborative effort between technologists, medical professionals, and sports scientists to ensure that the insights provided by wearables translate into actionable strategies that enhance player health and performance.

Adopting wearable technology also raises ethical considerations, particularly in terms of data privacy. Players must consent to share their data, and teams must ensure that this information is handled responsibly. Transparent data policies and robust security measures are essential to protect players' personal and health information. The balance between leveraging data for performance optimisation and maintaining players' privacy is delicate but crucial.

The future of wearable technology in cricket is promising but still evolving. As devices become more advanced and AI algorithms more sophisticated, the potential for even more precise injury prevention and management strategies will grow. Future innovations may include wearables that can diagnose injuries in real-time, offering instant recommendations for treatment. They might also provide even deeper insights into biomechanics, nutrition, and mental health, creating a comprehensive approach to player well-being.

Wearable technology has undeniably begun to revolutionise injury prevention and management in cricket. By providing real-time, personalised data, these devices enable a proactive approach to player health, reducing the risk of injuries while optimising performance. As technology continues to advance, the integration of AI and wearables will likely become an indispensable part of cricket, shaping the future of the sport in ways we are only just beginning to understand.

Predictive Modelling

In the relentless pursuit to keep cricketers at their peak, predictive modelling has emerged as a formidable ally in injury prevention and management. As the game continues to evolve, the stakes are undeniably high and the boundaries between human intuition and technological acumen are blurring. Predictive models, powered by sophisticated algorithms and vast datasets, offer a glimpse into potential futures, allowing teams and medical staff to pre-empt injuries before they cast a shadow over a player's career.

At its core, predictive modelling employs historical data coupled with real-time input to forecast probable injury scenarios. Each player's historical performance data, medical records, and even minute details like their biomechanics and physiological responses are fed into complex models. These models analyze patterns, recognizing precursors to injuries that might not be evident to the human eye.

Consider a fast bowler, for example. The intense physical strain they endure puts them at a high risk of injuries like stress fractures and muscle tears. By continuously monitoring their workload, bowling action, and even rest periods, predictive models can flag when their performance metrics stray into the danger zone. This proactive approach enables coaches to adjust training regimens, ensuring the bowler gets adequate recovery time to prevent injuries.

One compelling application of predictive modelling within cricket is the management of player workloads. High workloads without adequate recovery can lead to overuse injuries, a common issue in high-stakes, multi-format cricket. Using predictive analytics, teams can monitor players' cumulative workload and suggest optimal rest periods. Algorithms take into account various factors including match intensity, individual fitness levels, and recovery timelines, crafting a bespoke training and rest schedule that maximizes performance while minimizing injury risk.

Moving beyond the physical strain, predictive models also incorporate psychological factors. Mental fatigue often precedes physical breakdown, and models that factor in cognitive load can provide a more holistic injury prevention strategy. By tracking indicators of mental stress and fatigue, teams can tailor mental conditioning programs that mitigate the overall risk.

Moreover, wearable technology plays a crucial role in feeding real-time data into these predictive models. From GPS trackers to advanced accelerometers, wearables provide a deluge of data concerning a player's movements, acceleration, and exertion levels. This instant data flow ensures that predictive models are always working with the most current information, enhancing their accuracy and reliability. Imagine a scenario where a batsman's footwork shows subtle changes; the model, picking up these micro-adjustments, could forecast potential ankle strains, enabling preventive measures.

Another fascinating aspect of predictive modelling in cricket is the ability to customize injury prevention strategies on an individual level. Each player's anatomy and physiology are unique, and predictive models can create detailed profiles that map out specific injury risks based on an array of personal metrics. As a result, the medical staff can design bespoke programs that cater to individual needs, offering a level of personalization that was unimaginable just a few years ago.

Predictive modelling also excels in postoperative care and rehabilitation. Once a player sustains an injury, the road to recovery is fraught with challenges. Predictive models can aid in crafting precise rehabilitation protocols, forecasting recovery timelines, and suggesting the optimal exercises to ensure that players don't rush their comeback and risk re-injury.

The integration of vast datasets and advanced AI can sometimes feel like an impersonal touch in a highly personal sport, but it's important to remember that predictive modelling doesn't replace human expertise—it augments it. Medical and coaching staff remain integral to interpreting the data and making nuanced decisions that algorithms alone can't. The blend of machine learning capabilities with human insights creates a powerful, symbiotic relationship driving player safety and performance enhancements.

Looking forward, the technology underpinning predictive modelling is continually advancing. Machine learning techniques are getting more sophisticated, enabling better pattern recognition and more accurate predictions. The more data available, the sharper these models become. In the near future, we may see predictive models that not only prevent injuries but also forecast peak performance windows, helping management plan crucial fixtures with military precision.

From the veteran player steering towards the twilight of their career to the rookie just making their debut, predictive modelling provides invaluable insights that keep them on the field and at their best. The crucial takeaway is that predictive modelling is not just about avoiding injuries; it's about enabling players to sustain elite performance levels over longer periods.

A recent example underscores the impact predictive modelling can have. Consider a top international team that integrated predictive injury models into their routine. Over the season, they observed a significant reduction in injury rates, allowing them to field their best XI consistently. The strategic advantage conferred by having a fit and firing squad is enormous, often translating to better on-field results.

In summation, the intersection of artificial intelligence and sports, exemplified by predictive modelling, signifies a paradigm shift in injury prevention and management. This technology doesn't merely predict injuries; it revolutionizes how teams approach the health and availability of their players. In the high-octane world of cricket, where every match can be pivotal, the foresight offered by predictive modelling isn't just beneficial—it's indispensable.

As we continue to embrace these advancements, one can't help but feel a sense of awe at how far we've come, and a tingling excitement about where we're headed. Predictive modelling, with its myriad applications and ever-evolving prowess, promises to be a cornerstone in the ongoing quest to keep cricketers healthy, agile, and ready for the next big challenge.

Chapter 8:
Smart Decision-Making

As cricket evolves with the integration of artificial intelligence, smart decision-making emerges as a game-changer, redefining how teams strategize and execute plans on the field. Using AI-powered insights, teams can now make data-driven decisions, whether it's adjusting field placements in real-time or selecting the optimal batting order. This dynamic approach, driven by rapid data analysis, allows coaches and players to anticipate the opposition's moves, creating a more competitive and engaging match. Imagine a scenario where a bowler's deliveries are fine-tuned on the fly based on predictive models, or where a captain can instantly weigh the probabilities of various game outcomes. It's about harnessing the power of AI to make cricket not just a game of skill and endurance but also of smart, calculated strategies that bring a new level of depth to the sport.

On-Field Strategy

The cricket field is more than just a pitch; it's a complex battlefield where every decision can be the difference between triumph and defeat. When we talk about smart decision-making in cricket, we're not just focusing on pre-match preparations or post-match analyses. The essence of it lies in the moment—right there on the field, under the scorching sun or stadium lights. This is where artificial intelligence (AI) steps in, revolutionizing on-field strategy in ways that were once deemed the stuff of science fiction.

AI's role in on-field strategy begins with in-depth data analysis. By collecting and examining massive datasets, AI can predict outcomes and suggest strategies that aren't immediately obvious to the human eye. Imagine a bowler about to deliver his first ball to a new batsman. AI can provide insights into the batsman's weaknesses, past performances under similar conditions, and even suggest the optimal type of delivery. This level of precise information equips bowlers with the knowledge to outsmart their opponents, making every ball count.

Additionally, real-time data streaming enables an on-the-fly adjustment to the strategies. Coaches and analysts now have direct lines to vast AI databases during live matches. This means strategies can be tweaked in real-time based on unfolding scenarios. For instance, if a batting pair unexpectedly accelerates the run rate, AI can recommend optimal field placements and bowling changes almost instantaneously. This dynamic exchange of information significantly boosts the efficiency and success rate of decisions taken on the field.

Consider the role of AI in optimizing batting strategies. By analysing historical data, AI can identify patterns and tendencies of bowlers. Such insights inform batsmen about potential deliveries they might face and the types of shots that would be most effective. This doesn't just prepare batsmen mentally; it translates into practical, tactical decisions that improve performance. A well-prepped batsman is one who's not just playing to his strengths but is also exploiting the bowler's weaknesses.

Fielding, often an underappreciated aspect of cricket, is another area where AI shines. Advanced tracking systems can monitor players' movements, reaction times, and positioning. AI can then provide feedback to ensure optimal field placements, which is crucial for creating wicket-taking opportunities and restricting runs. Efficient fielding isn't about having the fastest runners or the best catchers alone; it's about putting those attributes in the right places at the right times.

Moreover, AI enables predictive modelling which is particularly useful when making strategic calls like deciding whether to bat or bowl first. By considering factors such as weather conditions, pitch report, and historical data, AI offers predictions on how the match might progress under given circumstances. It equips captains with the foresight to make more informed decisions, giving them an edge even before the first ball is bowled.

The psychological aspect of the game is another frontier AI is venturing into. Understanding an opponent's psychological state can tilt the balance in critical match situations. AI analyses can delve into players' past performances under pressure, providing insights into how likely they are to succeed in high-stakes scenarios. This information can be a game-changer in deciding when to introduce key bowlers or make strategic field changes during tense moments in the match.

Strategic use of AI can also enhance decision-making in line-up selections and on-field roles. Before the match even starts, AI can run simulations based on current form, fitness levels, and opposition analysis to suggest the most effective team composition. Once the players are on the field, AI assists in dynamic role assignments, such as determining when a particular bowler should be brought into the attack or identifying the right moment to switch batting positions to exploit specific bowlers.

Also, AI's ability to simulate various match situations allows teams to practice and prepare for different contingencies. Virtual simulations provide a safe environment for players to experiment with strategies and understand their impact without real-world consequences. This preparation enables players to handle unexpected situations more effectively during actual matches, as they have already encountered and resolved similar scenarios in simulations.

In high-pressure situations, when critical decisions need to be made rapidly, the human brain's cognitive load can sometimes hinder optimal decision-making. Here, AI can step in as an invaluable aid. For instance, in the final overs of a tight T20 match, when every run matters and every ball counts, AI tools can provide real-time analytics and actionable insights to assist the captain and the coaching staff in making the best possible decisions, possibly altering the outcome of the game in their favour.

AI's contribution to on-field strategy is not limited to professional teams alone. Amateur and grassroots cricket clubs are also beginning to harness AI's potential to refine their strategies and improve their game. This democratization of advanced technology has the power to elevate the quality of cricket at all levels and unearth talent that might have otherwise gone unnoticed.

The evolution of AI in cricket is much like the game itself—dynamic, unpredictable, and continually pushing the boundaries of what's possible. As AI continues to integrate deeper into the fabric of cricket, the way we think about on-field strategy will keep evolving. It's not just about data and numbers; it's about using that information to tell a story—a story of anticipation, strategy, and ultimately, success. The cricket field has always been a theatre of dreams, and with AI in play, those dreams are becoming smarter and more achievable every day.

Real-Time Adjustments

In the dynamic world of cricket, decisions made in the moment can be the difference between a thrilling victory and a heart-wrenching defeat. Enter AI, a technology revolutionising the game's very fabric by facilitating real-time adjustments that were previously the stuff of legend. By integrating real-time data analysis and AI capabilities, teams can now adapt on the fly with a level of precision and confidence that's unparalleled in the sport's history.

Already, we're seeing how AI interprets an array of on-field data—from player fatigue levels to pitch conditions and even weather changes—delivering insights to coaches and captains within moments. This immediacy allows for tactical shifts such as altering the bowling lineup, changing the field placements, or even suggesting batting strategies based on the historical performance of opposing players in similar conditions. The ability to make these swift modifications can drastically improve a team's adaptability and, consequently, its prospects in a match.

Let's examine field placements. AI can process countless variables in real-time to recommend the most effective positioning for fielders. It analyses the batting patterns of opponents, their scoring regions, and even the likelihood of certain shots. This predictive capability enables the fielding captain to place fielders in positions that maximise the chances of taking wickets or saving runs. Moreover, these recommendations aren't rigid; they evolve as the match progresses, ensuring that the team remains one step ahead.

Bowler rotations and match-up strategies have also benefited immensely from AI's real-time acumen. Historically, these decisions had been based largely on a captain's intuition and experience, which, while invaluable, are inherently limited by human cognition. In contrast, AI options are expansive and analytical, incorporating historical data and current game scenarios to suggest the best-suited bowler for each particular moment. If a bowler is showing signs of fatigue, AI can detect this early and recommend a timely switch, thereby preventing wear and enhancing performance.

Consider the case of injury management during matches. Smart wearable technology equipped with sensors can continuously monitor a player's physiological parameters. When these devices detect any signs of potential overexertion or injury risk, this real-time data is immediately flagged. Coaches and medical staff receive instant alerts, allowing them to act swiftly by substituting the player or advising modifications in their playing style to avoid worsening the condition. Thus, AI's role extends beyond strategic to the crucial, proactive preservation of player health.

Batting strategies can also be fine-tuned in real-time, thanks to AI. Batsmen can receive specific instructions pertinent to the bowler they're up against, including likely deliveries based on current match conditions and the bowler's pattern of play. This allows the batsman to adopt more calculated risks rather than relying solely on instinct. AI can suggest whether to play conservatively or aggressively, depending on variables like the required run rate and the remaining wickets, transforming how batting innings are approached and executed.

Real-time adjustments are particularly valuable under pressure situations where stakes are high, such as during the final overs of a tight T20 match or an intense Test match session. For instance, if a team needs to accelerate the run rate, AI can provide live updates on field changes and bowler fatigue, helping the batting team identify scoring opportunities. Conversely, when defending, AI assists in fine-tuning line and length for bowlers and adjusts the field to plug gaps effectively. This instantaneous feedback loop fosters an illusion of control amidst the apparent chaos, offering a competitive edge to the team that leverages these insights the best.

Beyond player and team-oriented decisions, AI's real-time adjustments also extend to umpiring and officiating. High-definition cameras and sophisticated algorithms work in tandem to review contentious decisions, ensuring that accurate and unbiased reviews can be made in seconds. This rapid, AI-driven adjudication process enhances the game's fairness and integrity, reducing controversies and improving the overall spectator experience.

The psychological advantage conferred by reliable AI support in real-time cannot be overstressed. Knowing that there's an additional layer of analytical insight backing their split-second decisions can bolster the captain's confidence and improve the morale of the entire team. It creates an environment where players feel more supported and strategically sound, thus enhancing their performance under pressure.

Real-time adjustments facilitated by AI also foster greater spectator engagement. Modern broadcasts integrate these analytics seamlessly, presenting them to viewers with visually appealing graphics and explanations. This not only enriches the viewing experience but also educates a broader audience about the subtleties and complexities of strategic decision-making in cricket. Fans gain a more in-depth understanding of the game, making their experience more immersive and intellectually stimulating.

The rapid evolution of AI technology promises even more sophisticated real-time adjustments in the future. With advancements in machine learning, pattern recognition, and predictive analytics, the precision and breadth of real-time decision-making will undoubtedly reach new heights. Teams that invest in and adeptly incorporate these tools will find themselves at a distinct advantage, elevating the entire standard of competitive cricket.

In conclusion, the incorporation of AI for real-time adjustments amounts to a paradigm shift in cricket. It impacts every facet of the game—from strategy formulation to in-the-moment tactical decisions—enhancing both the performance and safety of players. Whether through optimising field placements, managing bowler rotations, or preventing injuries, the profound capabilities of AI are transforming cricket into a smarter, more analytically driven sport. As technology continues to evolve, its ability to make split-second, informed adjustments will become an indispensable asset for any competitive team, redefining how the game is played and appreciated across the globe.

Chapter 9:
Player Scouting and Recruitment

In modern cricket, the journey from raw talent to professional star has become a scientific endeavour. Player scouting and recruitment have evolved dramatically, driven by the infusion of artificial intelligence (AI) into traditional methods. Gone are the days when talent scouts relied solely on intuition, hearsay, and rudimentary observations. Today, AI provides a granular, data-driven perspective that transforms how players are identified, evaluated, and ultimately recruited.

Traditional scouting methods relied on an experienced scout's ability to spot talent through physical prowess, technical skills, and instinctive gameplay. While seasoned scouts are invaluable, their perceptions can be subjective and prone to bias. AI brings objectivity and a level of analysis that human scouts simply can't match. Algorithms process vast amounts of data, offering insights into player performance metrics that are otherwise invisible to the human eye.

AI-driven scouting begins with extensive data collection. Every movement on the field, from a bowler's speed and spin to a batsman's shot accuracy, is captured through advanced sensors and cameras. This data is then processed to provide comprehensive profiles for each player. Through machine learning, algorithms identify patterns and trends that can predict a player's potential future performance. Clubs can analyse thousands of data points across multiple players, streamlining the selection process and reducing the risk of costly recruitment mistakes.

For instance, consider batting performance. AI scrutinises various aspects such as strike rate, ball type adaptability, and boundary-hitting capability. It evaluates players under different conditions, against various types of bowlers, and even at different stages of their careers. This meticulous analysis helps in identifying not just the top performers but also the underrated talents poised for a breakout. Teams equipped with such comprehensive data gain a competitive edge in recruitment decisions.

Bowling, too, benefits immensely from AI analytics. Modern cricketers must adapt to various formats—Test matches, One Day Internationals (ODIs), and Twenty20s (T20s). AI tracks bowlers over these formats, assessing their endurance, variation, and impact. Metrics such as economy rate, wicket-taking ability, and consistency are scrutinised to provide an exhaustive evaluation. Coaches and managers can rely on this data to make informed decisions and build a balanced team.

Moreover, fielding—often the unsung hero of cricket—is now analysed with precision. AI evaluates players' agility, reaction times, and accuracy in catching and throwing. Enhanced fielding can turn the tide in close matches, making these insights invaluable. Elite clubs recognise this, leveraging AI to scout players with exceptional fielding prowess alongside their batting or bowling skills.

The integration of AI also extends to psychological profiling. Cricket is as much a mental game as it is physical. Machine learning algorithms parse through behavioural data, social media activity, and even biometric feedback to gauge a player's mental toughness, temperament, and resilience under pressure. These psychological insights are pivotal in crafting a team that is not only skilled but also mentally resilient.

Consider a young bowler from a small village, away from the mainstream cricketing hubs. Traditional scouting might overlook his potential due to lack of exposure or opportunities. AI democratises this process by focusing purely on performance data. If the young bowler exhibits unique spin characteristics or an unusual, effective delivery, he won't remain unnoticed. AI ensures that genuine talent, irrespective of geography, gets the attention it deserves.

Similarly, AI is transforming how talent is nurtured at the grassroots level. Youth academies and local clubs can now leverage technology to identify budding talent early. AI's predictive models provide cues to develop specific skills, positioning young players for future success. This shifts focus from merely spotting talent to cultivating it systematically, ensuring a steady pipeline of skilled players ready for the professional arena.

AI-driven scouting also facilitates more dynamic recruitment strategies. Rather than focusing solely on established stars, clubs can adopt a portfolio approach—balancing between seasoned professionals and upcoming youngsters brimming with potential. This mix ensures sustainability and long-term success, reducing the reliance on high-stakes recruitment of well-known players.

Another revolutionary aspect is AI-assisted collaborative scouting. Clubs often work in silos, missing out on holistic views of a player's potential. Using centralized AI platforms, multiple clubs and academies can share data and insights, enriching the scouting ecosystem. With collaboration, everyone from local clubs to national selectors can access an extensive database, refining player evaluations and recruitment strategies across the board.

The international dimension of AI in scouting offers even broader horizons. Expanding beyond local leagues, data analytics can scout talent globally. Young cricketers from less prominent cricketing nations now have an avenue to showcase their skills. By casting a wider, data-driven net, AI enriches the talent pool, making global cricketing competitions more diverse and exciting.

While AI is a powerful tool, it doesn't replace the human element of scouting. Experienced scouts provide context that raw data cannot. They understand nuances like player relationships, chemistry, and cultural fit within the team. The symbiosis of AI data and human expertise creates a robust scouting mechanism. Scouts can validate AI findings, adding layers of insight that culminate in well-rounded recruitment decisions.

In conclusion, AI is setting unprecedented standards in player scouting and recruitment. From analysing detailed performance metrics to democratising talent identification, it's revolutionising how cricket teams are built. Detailed data analysis, psychological profiling, collaborative platforms, and global reach collectively shape a future where cricketing talent is more visible and accessible than ever. As AI continues to evolve, the possibilities for refining scouting and recruitment processes are boundless, promising a new era of cricketing excellence.

Chapter 10:
Opponent Analysis and
Strategy Formulation

In the intricate landscape of modern cricket, understanding your opponent is no longer a matter of intuition or hearsay. The advent of Artificial Intelligence (AI) has revolutionised how teams gather and interpret data, giving rise to a new era of opponent analysis and strategy formulation. This chapter delves into the transformative potential of AI in this regard, shedding light on how cricket teams are tapping into vast reservoirs of information to craft their game plans.

Historically, teams relied primarily on human scouts, past experiences, and basic statistical data to devise strategies. While effective to an extent, this approach was often riddled with limitations and subjective biases. Enter AI. Today, even the most granular details about an opponent's playing style, strengths, weaknesses, and behavioural patterns can be decoded with astonishing accuracy. Teams can access comprehensive datasets encompassing everything from batting averages in different conditions to bowlers' success rates against particular batsmen.

The crux of opponent analysis in cricket involves evaluating numerous facets—batting techniques, bowling strategies, field placements, and even psychological tendencies under pressure. AI excels in dissecting these components with unmatched precision. For instance, machine learning algorithms can scrutinise a batsman's footwork and predict susceptibility to particular deliveries. By aggregating and analysing video footage, AI can identify subtle hints that human observers might overlook.

Moreover, AI-powered tools can simulate match scenarios based on historical data. Virtual simulations allow coaches to experiment with various strategies against digital clones of their opponents. These simulations take into account myriad factors, including pitch conditions, weather forecasts, and player form. By immersing themselves in these simulated environments, teams can anticipate potential outcomes and refine their strategies accordingly.

Fundamentally, AI reduces the conjecture involved in strategy creation. Automated systems can process terabytes of data in mere seconds, offering actionable insights that are based on cold, hard facts rather than subjective interpretation. For example, if data reveals that a particular batsman struggles with outswingers delivered at a specific speed, bowlers can be trained to exploit this weak spot. Similarly, AI can aid in setting the most effective field placements to counter a batting line-up known for its proficiency with cover drives.

One notable tool in this AI-driven arsenal is pattern recognition. Advanced algorithms can identify recurring tactical patterns in an opponent's gameplay. Such patterns might go unnoticed by human analysts due to their subtlety or complexity, but AI can bring them to the fore with pinpoint clarity. Recognising these patterns can be pivotal in predicting how an opponent might react to various in-match scenarios, such as the different stages of an innings or shifting weather conditions.

In the realm of information sharing, AI also facilitates collaboration between international teams and domestic leagues. Cloud-based platforms enable seamless data exchange, allowing teams worldwide to benefit from each other's insights. This collective intelligence aids in creating comprehensive opponent profiles, making global cricket a more interconnected and strategically rich sport.

The dynamic nature of cricket necessitates that strategy formulation be both flexible and adaptive. Static, one-size-fits-all strategies are relics of the past. AI ensures that strategy formulation is an ongoing process, constantly evolving in response to real-time inputs. During matches, AI can provide live updates on key performance indicators, assist in making tactical adjustments, and offer recommendations for player substitutions based on predictive models.

Beyond the raw data and predictive models, AI also delivers psychological analysis. Through Natural Language Processing (NLP), AI can assess players' psychological states based on interviews, social media activity, and even their on-field demeanour. Understanding an opponent's mental framework allows teams to tailor their approaches, whether it's through sledging, strategic mind games, or displaying particular on-field behaviours to rattle key players.

It's essential to note that while AI is a powerful ally, it complements rather than replaces human expertise. Coaches, analysts, and players still play a crucial role in interpreting AI-generated data and insights. The blend of human intuition and machine intelligence forms the backbone of contemporary cricket strategy. This symbiotic relationship ensures that the final strategies are robust, nuanced, and contextualised.

Certainly, technology comes with its challenges. The implementation of AI in cricket strategy formulation requires significant investment in both financial and human resources. Teams need qualified data scientists, state-of-the-art software, and reliable data sources. Moreover, there is a learning curve associated with integrating AI systems into traditional coaching setups. Adaptation and adoption can sometimes be met with resistance from seasoned professionals who are accustomed to conventional methods.

Despite these challenges, the long-term benefits of AI in opponent analysis and strategy formulation are undeniable. Teams that have embraced AI report improved performance metrics, more coherent game plans, and a heightened ability to predict and counter opponent tactics. This success is not just limited to international cricket; domestic teams and even local clubs are beginning to integrate AI into their strategic arsenals.

As AI continues to evolve, its applications in opponent analysis are set to become even more sophisticated. Future developments might include more advanced machine learning models capable of mimicking the cognitive processes of top players, offering even deeper insights into opponent behaviour. Additionally, the rise of Internet of Things (IoT) devices could facilitate real-time player and equipment monitoring, feeding data back into AI systems for even more granular analysis.

In sum, AI has redefined the landscape of opponent analysis and strategy formulation in cricket. It offers a level of precision, adaptability, and insight that was previously unattainable. While the technology itself is complex, its end goal is simple: to give teams the edge they need to outthink, outmanoeuvre, and outperform their opponents. As cricket continues to evolve in this digital age, those who harness the power of AI will undoubtedly find themselves ahead of the curve.

Ultimately, the integration of AI into cricket exemplifies how tradition and technology can coalesce to enhance a sport that is universally cherished. Through meticulous opponent analysis and sophisticated strategy formulation, AI is not merely changing cricket; it is elevating it to unprecedented levels of strategic complexity and competitive intensity.

Chapter 11:
The Role of Big Data in Cricket

Cricket has always been a game of fine margins, where a single run, a single wicket, or even a single ball can change the course of a match. Historically, players and coaches relied heavily on intuition, experience, and rudimentary statistics. However, the evolution of big data has fundamentally transformed how the game is understood, played, and managed.

Big data refers to the immense volume of data generated from various sources, which can be analysed for insights that lead to better decision-making and strategic planning. In cricket, this means every ball bowled, shot played, or movement made on the field is captured, recorded, and analysed using advanced algorithms and machine learning techniques.

The utility of big data in cricket transcends beyond mere statistics. For instance, wearable technology provides real-time data on players' physical conditions. Every heartbeat, calorie burned, and muscle strain is monitored, adding a new dimension to injury prevention and fitness management. By crunching huge sets of data, teams can develop personalised training programs that optimise each player's performance.

Moreover, the role of big data extends into the realm of strategic planning. Before any game, teams delve deep into data analytics to understand their opponents' strengths and weaknesses. Detailed reports are generated, highlighting patterns such as a particular bowler's susceptibility to being hit in the death overs or a batsman's tendency to struggle against swing bowling in overcast conditions.

On match days, data-driven strategy becomes a real-time affair. Modern cricket teams employ data analysts who offer insights during the game. For example, feedback on field placements, bowling changes, and batting order rearrangements are often guided by real-time data analysis. This dynamic approach of marrying historical data with real-time data offers a competitive edge that's hard to match.

One of the standout contributions of big data in cricket is the advent of advanced performance metrics. Traditional metrics like batting average and strike rate have been expanded to include zones of efficiency, strike rate under pressure, and expected runs based on pitch conditions. These advanced metrics create a more holistic understanding of a player's contribution and potential, enabling teams to make more informed selections and tactical decisions.

Performance metrics generated through big data aren't confined to professional cricketers alone. Aspiring players at the grassroots level and amateurs can benefit from these insights. Subscription-based platforms and apps allow individuals to track their performances, receive guidance, and thus, enhance their skillsets, levelling the playing field.

Another area where big data has made a significant impact is in player scouting and recruitment. Teams are no longer reliant on anecdotes and manual scouting reports. Instead, scouts use massive datasets to identify hidden talents. Data points like performance in domestic circuits, adaptability to different playing conditions, and even psychological resilience can be quantified, ensuring a more thorough vetting process.

Supporters and enthusiasts, too, gain access to a treasure trove of information. Real-time statistics, player comparisons, and predictive models enrich the viewing experience, making it more interactive and engaging. Fans can engage in informed discussions, understand the game's nuances, and appreciate the strategic depth involved in cricket.

Interestingly, the benefits of big data extend beyond the boundary ropes. Cricket boards and franchise owners can leverage extensive datasets for business intelligence. Analyses of consumer behaviour, ticket sales, and social media trends inform marketing strategies and fan engagement initiatives. By tailoring experiences to meet fan expectations, cricket has transitioned into a more fan-centric sport.

Challenges, however, do accompany these advancements. Data privacy and the ethical use of player information are hotly debated topics. Ensuring data security and establishing clear guidelines on data ownership and consent becomes paramount in a landscape where data is the new gold.

Moreover, while data analytics provides remarkable insights, the human element shouldn't be undermined. Qualitative observations, instinct, and experience still play crucial roles in cricket. Balancing data-driven strategies with human judgement will ensure the game retains its intrinsic charm and unpredictability.

Yet, the future of cricket appears poised for further intertwining with big data. Predictive analytics, already in use, will become more refined, allowing for accurate predictions not just on the field but off it as well. This is where artificial intelligence and big data converge, offering unprecedented capabilities in forecasting player potential, match outcomes, and even injury risks.

In essence, big data in cricket is not merely a tool—it's a transformative force. It allows for a deeper, more nuanced understanding of the game, offering a competitive edge to teams that adapt to this data-rich environment. From performance enhancement to strategic advantages, and from fan engagement to operational efficiencies, the role of big data in cricket is both profound and multi-dimensional. It's an exciting time to be involved in the sport, as the confluence of tradition and technology opens new horizons for players, teams, and fans alike.

Chapter 12:
AI in Umpiring and Decision Review System (DRS)

The advent of artificial intelligence in cricket has made resourceful interventions, but perhaps none stand out more strikingly than in the realm of umpiring and the Decision Review System (DRS). Long gone are the days when the fate of a game rested solely on human perception, which is inherently fallible. While every cricket enthusiast loves the spirit of the game, it's equally crucial to ensure that the decisions made on the field are as accurate as possible. Enter AI.

Umpiring in cricket is an immense responsibility. One wrong call can change the flow of the game—a no-ball missed, a close lbw (leg before wicket) decision, or a catch that goes unnoticed. AI's incorporation into DRS seeks to bridge the gap between human error and technological precision. The result? A fairer, more transparent game that caters to its players and audience. It's a paradigm shift that's recalibrating the traditional narratives of cricket.

One of the key contributions of AI to umpiring is ball-tracking technology, commonly referred to as Hawk-Eye. The system uses multiple high-speed cameras positioned around the field to track the ball's trajectory. These cameras feed data into software that creates a 3D representation of the ball's path, allowing umpires to make informed decisions on lbw appeals and other contentious points. The ball-tracking system not only accounts for the pitch of the ball but also predicts its direction post-impact, making it an invaluable tool in the umpire's arsenal.

Snickometer, another breakthrough powered by AI, detects faint edges that the human ear might miss. When a batsman supposedly edges the ball but the sound is too subtle to catch, Snickometer steps in. Utilising a sensitive microphone placed on the stumps, this system picks up even the faintest of sounds and produces a visual representation, helping umpires make crucial decisions. It's moments like these where AI showcases its ability to revolutionise cricket umpiring, preserving the game's integrity by leveraging technological finesse.

Hot Spot technology, widely recognised for its use in detecting edges and bat-pad catches, employs infra-red imaging to identify areas of the bat or pads that have been struck by the ball. When seen through the lens of AI, Hot Spot stands out as a beacon of innovative umpiring. The infra-red cameras capture the heat generated by the friction between bat or pad and ball, which is then displayed as a glowing spot on a monochromatic image. This system, though not entirely devoid of flaws, acts as another layer of decision-making support, reducing the margin of error.

The Decision Review System itself is a testament to the fusion of AI and cricket. Allowing players to challenge on-field decisions, DRS makes use of all aforementioned technologies—Hawk-Eye, Snickometer, and Hot Spot—to validate or overturn decisions. This multi-faceted approach increases the reliability of reviews, ensuring that justice is served on the field. DRS has its critics, but there is no denying its positive impact on the game, minimising disputes and letting the cricketing action shine.

To understand the impact of AI in umpiring, one must consider the case of "umpire's call". When the ball-tracking technology shows that the ball is clipping the stumps, but not firmly enough to overturn the on-field umpire's decision, 'umpire's call' is invoked. This rule acknowledges the inherent uncertainties in any predictive system while still offering a technological perspective. It's a balance between human intuition and mechanical precision, emphasising the collaborative potential between umpires and AI.

AI has also enriched the umpire's role in real-time decision-making. Traditionally, the third umpire had to rely on replay footage to make decisions on run-outs and stumpings. With AI, the process is expedited. Algorithms can quickly sift through multiple camera angles, apply object detection to identify the precise moments of interest, and even assist in ruling without much time lag. This not only streamlines the process but also reduces the pressure on human umpires, allowing them to focus better on the game's live aspects.

For all its advancements, the implementation of AI in umpiring hasn't been without its share of challenges. One primary concern is the dependency on technology, which can malfunction or yield inconclusive data. Moreover, there's the human element—players and fans sometimes resist technology, feeling it detracts from the human spirit of the sport. Such sentiments resulted in debates about whether DRS should be standardised across all formats and matches or remain selectively applied.

Despite these challenges, the potential benefits outweigh the drawbacks. Continuous improvements in AI algorithms and technology promise even greater accuracy and reliability, ensuring that these systems evolve alongside the demands of modern cricket. Developers are creating more refined versions of ball-tracking technology, and machine learning models are becoming increasingly adept at analysing intricate movements and minute details, thus further reducing the likelihood of erroneous decisions.

In perspective, AI in umpiring and DRS signifies the blending of tradition with innovation. Cricket has always been a sport rich in history, its tales and legends passed down generations. Integrating AI into this narrative doesn't erase its essence; it enhances it. Fans can now trust that the game's outcome is governed by the closest approximation of fairness and accuracy possible.

This technological marriage also provides a framework for other sports to emulate. Cricket's pioneering use of AI in decision-making tasks sets a precedent, encouraging other major sports like football, tennis, and even baseball to integrate similar technologies. It's an inspiration, showing how a sport anchored in tradition can courageously manoeuvre into the future.

Players, too, benefit from this paradigm shift. With AI support, they can focus on their skill and strategy without the lingering doubt of potential umpiring errors. Knowing that contentious decisions can be reviewed and accurately judged instils a sense of fairness, which is crucial for mental preparation and performance. AI is thus a leveller, providing a more equitable ground for competition.

In closing, AI's role in umpiring and DRS is undoubtedly transformative. It hasn't just altered how decisions are reviewed but has recalibrated the entire conception of fairness in this cherished sport. By harnessing AI, cricket ensures it doesn't just keep up with technological progress but sets benchmarks for it. As we move forward, AI will only become more ingrained in cricket, bringing with it the promise of precision, fairness, and the undying spirit of the game.

Chapter 13:
Enhancing Fan Engagement

Transforming how cricket fans interact with the game, artificial intelligence is reshaping the landscape of sports engagement. By leveraging AI-powered analyses and personalised content, fans are now experiencing cricket in unprecedented ways. Imagine receiving real-time statistics mid-match tailored to your favourite players or predictive insights on match outcomes that keep you on the edge of your seat. This level of interaction isn't just about following a score but immersing oneself in a dynamic, data-rich experience that deepens one's connection to the game. AI algorithms are also fostering a sense of community among fans by curating content that resonates on an individual level, making the entire spectator experience highly interactive and deeply personal. As AI continues to evolve, it promises to make cricket not only more accessible but also profoundly engaging, ensuring that fans feel more connected and passionate than ever before.

AI-Powered Analyses

When it comes to enhancing fan engagement, AI-powered analyses stand at the forefront of this transformative experience. Imagine being able to understand a player's performance down to the minutest detail, not just through traditional statistics but through intricate data points and models driven by artificial intelligence. This level of insight is no longer a futuristic ideal; it's the current reality reshaping how fans interact with the game of cricket.

What used to be limited to on-field performances and post-match highlights has remarkably evolved into an intricate ballet of numbers and predictions. Through machine learning algorithms, AI can process vast datasets to offer in-depth analyses, enriching the viewer's understanding of every ball bowled and every shot played. This isn't just limited to surface-level metrics; it delves deeper into predictive analytics, showcasing potential outcomes based on past performances and situational variables.

Consider a scenario where a bowler consistently struggles against left-handed batsmen. A fan equipped with this AI-driven insight will not only expect a particular strategy but also understand the reasoning behind it. This advanced knowledge elevates the viewing experience from passive observation to active engagement. Each delivery becomes a part of a broader narrative, making every moment on the field more exciting and consequential.

Let's delve deeper into how AI-powered analyses are redefining the cricketing experience:

- *Fan Prediction Models:* AI enables fans to become analysts themselves. With predictive models, they can forecast individual and team performances, adding an extra layer of personal engagement.

- *Performance Breakdown:* By breaking down performances into granular data points, fans can appreciate the intricacies of cricket in new ways. This includes insights into batting techniques, bowling patterns, and even fielding placements.

- *Real-Time Insights:* AI-powered platforms can offer real-time analyses, allowing fans to understand the strategic decisions being made. This instant feedback loop keeps fans glued to the match, making every play vital.

These AI-powered models aren't just confined to professional analysts or commentators; they are accessible to the general audience through various applications and platforms. This democratization of data brings the average fan into the analytical fold, empowering them with the same tools that professional coaches and players use.

A significant consequence of this enhanced engagement is the sense of community and competition it fosters among fans. Predictive analytics and AI-driven insights naturally lend themselves to fantasy cricket leagues, where fans can form teams, predict outcomes, and compete against each other based on real-time data. This not only heightens their engagement with the sport but also transforms their understanding of the game's dynamics.

AI-powered analyses also offer personalised highlights tailored to individual viewing preferences. Suppose a fan is particularly interested in a player's batting style. In that case, algorithms can curate specific video segments that focus on that player's performance, dissecting each movement and decision. This personalised content makes each fan's experience unique and more aligned with their interests.

Moreover, on social media platforms, AI analyses can drive discussions and debates among fans, enriching the collective viewing experience. By wielding the ability to verify or question on-field decisions and strategies, fans become more knowledgeable and passionate advocates for their teams. This shift from being mere spectators to informed participants enhances their connection to the sport and each other.

The analytical prowess of AI doesn't just stop at enhancing the fan experience during the matches. It extends to post-match analyses, allowing fans to dive deep into performances, dissecting each player's contribution with an almost forensic level of detail. This level of engagement encourages a more profound appreciation of the skills and strategies involved in cricket.

Given the rise in the accessibility and sophistication of AI tools, it's not surprising that cricket boards and broadcasters are investing heavily in integrating AI-powered analyses into their offerings. By enriching live broadcasts with AI-driven insights, they provide augmented experiences that capture the imagination and interest of a broader audience base.

The intertwining of live action with advanced data analytics also opens avenues for educating newer fans about the sport's complexities. Newcomers often find cricket's intricate rules and strategies daunting. AI's capability to offer real-time explanations and context transforms the learning curve into a fascinating journey of discovery. This democratization of knowledge makes cricket more accessible and engaging for everyone, irrespective of their level of familiarity with the sport.

The broader cultural impact of AI-powered analyses in cricket shouldn't be understated. By providing detailed, quantitative insights, AI enables the sport to transcend traditional narratives and enter discussions typically dominated by data-centric fields. This convergence between sport and data science fosters a new kind of cricket enthusiast, one who appreciates the game for both its athleticism and its analytical depth.

Clearly, AI-powered analyses are not just auxiliary features; they represent a fundamental shift in how fans interact with cricket. The depth and breadth of data available transform every match into an opportunity for discovery and engagement. Far from being passive consumers, fans are now co-participants in the analytical process, making each moment of the game richer and more satisfying.

To truly appreciate the impact of AI in cricket, consider a world without these advancements. Matches would revert to simpler interpretations, rich in tradition but perhaps lacking the nuanced understanding that AI brings. While nostalgia has its place, the forward march of technology depicts a more informed, engaged, and enthusiastic fanbase, one ready to delve into the sport's evolving complexities.

In conclusion, AI-powered analyses represent a seismic shift in how fans engage with cricket. The integration of AI into the fan experience not only deepens their understanding of the sport but redefines what it means to be a fan. As artificial intelligence continues to evolve, one can only imagine the new heights of engagement and excitement that await cricket enthusiasts around the world.

Personalised Content

In the grand tapestry of cricket, perhaps what stitches the players and the action tightly to the hearts of fans is the sense of personal connection. Technology, and more specifically artificial intelligence (AI), has revolutionised how this connection is not only formed but enhanced. Through personalised content curated for each fan, AI has transformed the viewer's experience from a passive to an actively engaging one.

Imagine a fan waking up in London, her phone lighting up with notifications highlighting the key plays of her favourite team from a match that took place overnight in New Zealand. Not only that, but these highlights have been meticulously chosen based on her past viewing habits, ensuring she doesn't miss a moment that would get her pulse racing. This is the magic of personalised content, and it is only the beginning.

In contrast to generic content that is distributed en masse, personalised content tailors every piece of information to the individual. It's like having a dedicated concierge service for cricket. Fans today are flooded with information, and the bombardment can be overwhelming. AI sifts through massive troves of data to deliver personalised highlights, player interviews, and match analyses that are most relevant to each person's interests.

For instance, seasoned fans who are deeply interested in the intricacies of the game might receive detailed analysis of a bowler's technique, complete with slow-motion breakdowns and expert commentary. Meanwhile, casual viewers might get snappy, exciting match highlights designed to keep them entertained without diving too deeply into the details. This differentiation is made possible by machine learning algorithms that analyse viewing patterns and preferences.

Moreover, AI-powered platforms can learn and adapt. Each interaction, each clicked video, each read article enhances the AI's understanding of a fan's preferences. Over time, the platform evolves, becoming more adept at delivering exactly what the fan wants. This creates a more engaging and satisfying experience for fans, almost ensuring their loyalty.

Audience engagement also reaches new heights with personalised recommendations for live match experiences. AI can notify fans about upcoming matches that feature their favourite players or teams, even suggesting optimal times to purchase tickets based on availability and price fluctuations. In such ways, AI doesn't just show fans what happened; it brings them into the fold, making them feel an integral part of the cricketing world.

Personalised content extends beyond videos and articles. Social media platforms, applications, and websites today utilise AI to create an engaging and interactive environment for fans. Through these platforms, fans may receive personalised messages from their favourite players, based on AI simulations that predict what would make a particular fan feel special. Imagine getting a birthday wish from your favourite cricketer, tailored to include your favourite cricket moments and achievements. Such experiences deepen the emotional connection and enhance fan loyalty.

Furthermore, AI can personalise the way statistics and data are presented. A tech-savvy reader might prefer raw data, graphs, and in-depth reports, while another might enjoy animated statistics that are easier to digest but still insightful. Customized dashboards allow fans to choose what kind of data presentations they wish to see, enhancing both engagement and satisfaction.

One dynamic example comes from interactive apps that offer predictive insights during a live match, prompting fans to engage even more. For example, an app might alert a fan that a certain bowler usually bowls a game-changing over in the death-overs, prompting anticipation and excitement. These insights would be based on historical data and real-time analysis, shifting the fan experience from just watching to predicting and interacting.

Augmented Reality (AR) features powered by AI can also provide immersive experiences. Imagine putting on a headset and watching a holographic representation of a player's signature move right in your living room. The AI understands which player you're most excited about and directs the AR experience accordingly. In this way, modern technology is not just enhancing how much content is delivered, but how intimately it can be experienced.

Gaming experiences have also evolved thanks to AI and personalised content. Apps and platforms that allow fans to create fantasy teams based on real-time data have surged in popularity. AI ensures that fans receive player recommendations based on up-to-the-minute statistics, injury reports, and even weather conditions. This highly personalised approach ensures that every gaming session is as engaging as it is competitive.

From player-themed quizzes to personalised newsletters containing in-depth match reports, the scope of personalised content is broad and constantly expanding. Every section of a news website, every corner of a sports app can be finetuned to reflect the reader's preferences. This ensures fans always find exactly what they are looking for, making their interaction with the sport deeply satisfying.

Additionally, AI-powered voice assistants are making their mark. These assistants can provide instant updates on ongoing matches, answer trivia questions, and even provide pre-match and post-match summaries—all tailored to what they know the fan enjoys. Just by talking to a device, fans can trigger a cascade of personalised content, making their engagement with the sport seamless and effortless.

The ultimate goal of these AI systems is to create a feedback loop of engagement—where personalised content keeps fans interested, and their interactions further refine the AI's ability to deliver even more engaging content. The circle of interaction ensures that the relationship between a fan and the sport remains dynamic and fulfilling.

Looking toward the future, the possibilities are endless. As AI becomes more sophisticated, the level of personalisation will only deepen. Future advancements could include holographic projections of live matches right in one's living room or virtual reality environments customised based on a fan's historical interests. The horizon is bright, and it promises a richer, more interactive engagement with cricket than ever before.

Chapter 14:
Virtual and Augmented Reality

As we navigate the terrain of artificial intelligence in cricket, it becomes imperative to explore the frontiers of virtual and augmented reality. These technologies hold the potential to fundamentally alter our experience and understanding of the game. From immersive training environments to enhanced fan experiences, virtual and augmented reality (VR and AR) are set to redefine how cricket is played, watched, and analysed.

Virtual reality in cricket can be visualised as a high-fidelity, simulated environment that allows players and coaches to immerse themselves in a digital replica of the playing field. Imagine a cricketer donning a VR headset and finding themselves in a simulated match situation. They could practice their response to a range of deliveries and match conditions, from facing fast bowlers on a green top to tackling spinners on a turning track. The possibilities are limitless. By providing players with realistic and repeatable practice scenarios, VR ensures that each session is as beneficial as possible, without the constraints of weather, physical wear, or other logistical concerns.

In the realm of augmented reality, the game's physical aspect integrates seamlessly with digital overlays. Think of AR glasses worn by spectators at the stadium, providing real-time statistics, player information, and even replay highlights right in their field of vision. It's not just about enhancing viewing pleasure but also about delivering a layer of interactivity that traditional broadcasting simply can't match.

For coaches, VR serves as a dynamic tool to enhance strategic planning. They can hold virtual match previews where players experience simulated game scenarios, helping them better understand their roles and responsibilities. For instance, a bowler could practice different strategies for a specific batsman they will face in an upcoming match. This hands-on experience can be invaluable when it comes to making split-second decisions on the field.

Augmented reality can also upgrade the live viewing experience. Fans at home or in the stadium could use AR devices or apps to overlay statistical data, heat maps, and predictive models directly onto the live footage. Imagine watching a match and instantly seeing the predicted trajectory of a ball bowled by a fast bowler or the heat map indicating a batsman's favourite scoring areas. It's a powerful way to keep audiences engaged and informed, enhancing their understanding and enjoyment of the game.

Moreover, these technologies have the promise of democratizing access to high-quality training resources. For young cricketers and amateur players, VR can serve as an entry point to professional-level coaching without requiring physical presence at elite training facilities. They can encounter match-like situations, receive feedback, and refine their skills from the comfort of their homes. Augmented reality can transform simple backyard cricket; youngsters could receive real-time coaching tips as they play, helping them mimic the techniques of their cricketing idols.

One of the more intriguing prospects of AR in cricket lies in its integration with wearable technology. Imagine a smart helmet that provides cricketers with real-time data about ball speed, predicted bounce, and even the potential swing. By supplementing traditional instinctive play with actionable data, players can make more informed decisions on the fly, potentially improving their performance.

The impact of VR and AR in fan engagement can't be overstated. Picture yourself being transported to a virtual cricket museum, exploring the rich history of the game, interacting with life-sized holograms of cricket legends, and experiencing iconic moments through immersive 360-degree videos. This not only brings fans closer to the sport but also enhances their appreciation for its legacy.

From an analytical perspective, virtual and augmented reality can facilitate deeper insights into player performance. Analysts can review match scenarios in virtual environments, dissect tactics, and even run simulations to explore the outcomes of different strategies. This analytical depth enables a more comprehensive understanding of the game, equipping coaches and players with nuanced insights that can translate to on-field success.

Implementing VR and AR technologies isn't without its challenges. High production costs, technological barriers, and the need for extensive training for users are among the hurdles. However, as these technologies become more accessible and integrated into the cricketing ecosystem, their potential benefits far outweigh the initial investment. The scalability of VR and AR solutions means they could soon become commonplace, from grassroots cricket to international arenas.

Despite the technological advancements, the essence of cricket remains unchanged. These innovations are tools to enhance the understanding, training, and enjoyment of the game, not to replace its core spirit. The human element of cricket—the instincts, the reactions, the emotional highs and lows—will always be central to the sport. VR and AR aim to enrich these facets, not overshadow them.

In conclusion, virtual and augmented reality promise a future where the boundaries between the physical and digital realms blur. This convergence stands to transform how the game is played, coached, and experienced. Embracing these technologies will enable cricketers, coaches, and fans to remain at the cutting edge, ensuring cricket evolves with the times while preserving its timeless appeal. As we look ahead, the fusion of VR and AR with artificial intelligence heralds an exciting era where cricket is not just a sport but an immersive, interactive experience that engages all senses.'

Chapter 15:
AI in Cricket Broadcasting

Imagine a cricket match where every ball, every swing of the bat, and every strategic move is not just watched, but dissected and presented with a richness of detail previously unimaginable. That's the magic AI brings to cricket broadcasting. This technology redefines commentary, providing insights that elevate the viewer's understanding and enjoyment of the game. Enhanced visual analytics, augmented by AI, deliver real-time stats, predictive models for future plays, and detailed performance analytics. The marriage of AI and broadcasting turns a cricket match into an immersive experience, making fans feel like they're part of the strategy room. With dynamic overlays, intelligent replays, and AI-driven commentary, watching cricket becomes an interactive narrative, not just a passive pastime. AI not only makes cricket broadcasts more informative and engaging but also transforms how fans connect with the sport they love.

Commentary Enhancement

In the evolving world of cricket broadcasting, the role of commentary has transformed significantly, driven by advancements in artificial intelligence (AI). Historically, commentary relied heavily on the experience and intuition of seasoned commentators. However, AI now brings a layer of analytical insight and real-time data processing, offering a richer and more engaging experience for viewers.

Imagine a cricket match where commentary is not just about narrating the live action but also providing detailed insights into player form, historical data, and predictive analyses. AI-driven commentaries can continuously update and present statistics in ways that help viewers understand the nuances of the game in real-time. This fusion of traditional narrative and advanced analytics is changing the way fans consume cricket.

Mainstream broadcasters have started integrating AI technologies to enhance the capabilities of commentators. With real-time data analysis, AI helps commentators deliver more precise and impactful insights. For instance, the data generated from AI can inform why a particular bowler is likely to take a wicket, based not just on current form but also on minute details such as the batsman's weaknesses and environmental conditions.

Moreover, AI commentary enhancement allows for a personalised experience for different viewers. AI can cater to various levels of cricket knowledge, from beginners to hardcore statisticians. By leveraging machine learning algorithms, the commentary can adapt its complexity and detail, ensuring that every viewer feels engaged and informed.

Natural language processing (NLP), a subset of AI, plays a crucial role in this commentary transformation. NLP models can process vast amounts of cricketing data and generate natural, context-aware language that sounds remarkably human. These models not only provide statistical data but also weave them into compelling narratives that keep viewers hooked.

Additionally, AI aids in predicting moments of high excitement, helping commentators build anticipation. AI can analyse historical patterns and current game data to signal potential turning points, alerting commentators to heighten their narrative around key moments. This predictive element adds an extra layer of drama and engagement, making the broadcast experience richer.

Commentators are no longer isolated figures but part of an interconnected web of data and analysis, feeding off AI-generated insights to deliver commentary that's more informative and cohesive. When a commentator talks about a batting strategy, the AI can concurrently display visual analytics on screen, supporting the verbal commentary with graphical data, thus creating a multi-layered narrative.

One of the exciting features AI brings to commentary is the ability to spot subtle trends that human observers might miss. For instance, AI can flag when a particular bowler starts to exhibit signs of fatigue, backing this observation with metrics like reduced ball speed, less spin, or changes in accuracy. This insight allows commentators to make nuanced comments that enrich the viewing experience.

Inclusivity is another important dimension where AI-powered commentary shines. AI systems can deliver commentary in multiple languages simultaneously, enabling a broader audience to enjoy the game in their native tongue. This technological leap fosters global unity through sports, making cricket accessible to more fans across different regions and languages.

Interactive features brought about by AI enhancements in commentary are also worth noting. Viewers can now engage with the commentary by voting for what analyses they want to see next or asking real-time questions to AI-powered virtual commentators. This interaction makes the viewing experience more immersive and participatory.

Commentary systems empowered by AI have capabilities that extend beyond real-time game analysis. They can provide historical context with unprecedented accuracy and depth. Whether it's comparing a current player's performance to legends of the past or recalling memorable match moments from years ago, AI ensures that the commentary is always relevant and engaging.

Sentiment analysis, another facet of AI, can gauge public reaction and feed it into the commentary. By analysing social media trends and fan chatter, AI can highlight what aspects of the game are capturing the audience's imagination, allowing commentators to address these talking points effectively. This creates a more connected and responsive viewing experience.

AI-enhanced commentary also offers significant benefits for training and development. Aspiring commentators can use AI tools to hone their skills, practicing with AI simulations that provide real-time feedback. This ensures a continuous influx of well-trained, knowledgeable commentators who can elevate the broadcast experience.

The future of AI in cricket commentary holds exciting prospects. As AI technology continues to evolve, so will its capacity to deliver insightful, engaging, and interactive commentary. We're on the cusp of a new era where AI doesn't just supplement human commentary but synergizes with it to create a compelling viewer experience that was previously unimaginable.

However, the integration of AI in commentary isn't without its challenges. Balancing the human touch with AI's analytical precision is crucial. The charm of cricket commentary lies in its human warmth, the anecdotes, and the spontaneous reactions. Ensuring AI complements and enhances rather than overshadows human commentators will be a delicate balancing act.

Yet, the potential rewards far outweigh the challenges. The marriage of AI and cricket commentary promises to democratise cricket knowledge, making very complex tactical analyses accessible to everyday fans. In a sport where even minor details can significantly alter outcomes, the granularity of AI-generated insights is a game-changer.

Furthermore, the scalability of AI means that the same high-quality commentary experiences can be delivered across multiple platforms, from traditional TV broadcasts to streaming services and even social media. This consistency ensures that fans get top-notch commentary no matter how they choose to watch the game.

AI's role in enhancing cricket commentary is a testament to how technology can enrich traditional practices by making them more dynamic and impactful. As we advance, the boundary between human intuition and machine intelligence in sports broadcasting will continue to blur, offering fans an enhanced, engaging, and highly personalised experience.

In summation, AI is not just enhancing cricket commentary; it is revolutionising it. By providing real-time data, predictive insights, and personalisation, AI turns commentary into a rich tapestry of analysis and narrative. This technological transformation ensures that the beauty and intricacies of cricket are communicated more effectively, bringing fans closer to the action than ever before.

Visual Analytics

The world of cricket broadcasting has transformed remarkably with the advent of artificial intelligence, and at the heart of this evolution lies visual analytics. This powerful tool leverages vast amounts of data to offer more than just a simple viewing experience; it creates an immersive, informative, and interactive engagement that demystifies the complexities of the game. Visual analytics in cricket combines statistical data with dynamic graphics, providing a layered comprehension of events unfolding on the field.

From heat maps indicating players' movements to tracking the trajectory of the ball in real time, visual analytics opens a window into aspects of the game that were previously opaque. Imagine a batsman's wagon wheel—an iconic graphic that displays the direction in which the batsman has hit the ball. Enhanced by AI, this graphic can now show not just the direction but the speed of each hit, the type of shot played, and the bowler faced. Such detailed insights provide commentators with rich, contextual data to engage and educate viewers.

The detail doesn't stop at the individual level. Team dynamics can also be interpreted through visual analytics. Cluster graphs, for example, can display fielding positions relative to various batsmen, spotlighting strategic decisions. In the hands of expert commentators, this type of analysis translates into a deeper understanding for the audience, who can then see the rationale behind every tactical move.

In real-time broadcasts, predictive modeling powered by AI is revolutionising how fans anticipate the outcome of the game. Win probability graphs, which dynamically update as the match progresses, offer a vivid narrative flow. As each ball is bowled and every run scored or wicket taken, these graphs adjust to reflect the changing fortunes of the teams, adding a layer of suspense and excitement.

Visual analytics also serves as a tool for better storytelling. Cricket is a game rich in narratives, from rivalries to underdog victories. Heat maps can highlight a bowler's "hot zones"—areas where they are most effective. They can also show a batsman's strengths and weaknesses against different types of deliveries. These elements combine to create stories that captivate the audience, bringing statistical data to life in a compelling format.

Moreover, the use of AI-driven visual analytics enhances accessibility and understanding for new fans. Cricket, with its myriad rules and strategies, can be overwhelming for newcomers. By breaking down complex data into simple, visual forms, AI makes the game more approachable. Novice viewers can easily grasp the essentials, like why a particular field setting is employed or how a batsman's style adapts to different bowlers.

One of the most impressive advancements is the integration of augmented reality (AR) with visual analytics. Through AR, broadcasters can superimpose graphical data directly onto the live feed. Techniques like Hawk-Eye, for instance, show ball trajectories and umpiring decisions in augmented reality, making it far easier for viewers to understand on-field decisions. This blending of real-time data with visual representation enriches the viewing experience exponentially.

Interactive dashboards are another facet of visual analytics that have captured the imagination of cricket fans. These dashboards allow viewers to interact with various data points during the game. They can pull up stats on players, see historical data, and even compare team performances. This interactive element turns passive viewership into an active experience, engaging fans on a whole new level and allowing them to dive deep into data they find most interesting.

We've also seen a rise in personalised content delivery, driven by visual analytics. AI algorithms can track viewing habits and preferences, tailoring the broadcast to individual tastes. Fans interested in batting can receive more in-depth analysis on batsmen, while those intrigued by bowling can delve into bowlers' strategies and their effectiveness. This personalisation not only enhances viewer satisfaction but also cultivates a more engaged and loyal audience base.

Another compelling application is the use of visual analytics in historical comparisons. Fans love to compare current players with legends of the past, and AI-driven visuals can make these comparisons vivid and factual. Performance bar charts can juxtapose the batting averages of contemporary players with those from different eras, facilitating a deeper appreciation of the evolution of the game.

The integration of drones and high-definition cameras has added yet another layer to visual analytics in cricket broadcasting. These technologies provide aerial views and intricate angles that were previously impossible. Combined with AI, they can analyse ball spin, bounce, and swing with unparalleled accuracy. With high-definition slow-motion replays, viewers can appreciate every minute detail, from the ball glancing off the edge of the bat to the exact moment a fielder makes a catch.

Fans aren't the only ones benefiting from these advancements. Coaches and analysts use these rich visuals to fine-tune strategies and improve players' performances. By reviewing visual analytics, they can identify areas needing improvement and formulate specific drills to address them. This analytical depth informs training methodologies, resulting in more refined skills and better on-field performances.

The integration of AI in broadcasting doesn't just enrich live matches but extends to pre- and post-match analyses. Using visual analytics, experts can dissect team performances, isolate key moments that influenced the game, and provide predictive insights for future encounters. This thorough breakdown aids teams in refining their strategies while offering fans a comprehensive understanding of the game's ebb and flow.

These advancements are not merely limited to professional cricket. Amateur and grassroots levels are also benefitting from AI-driven visual analytics. Young players can access the same level of detailed analysis to understand their strengths and areas for improvement. Clubs and coaches can employ these tools to foster talent from a young age, ensuring a higher standard of play as these athletes advance through the ranks.

In summary, visual analytics has truly revolutionised cricket broadcasting. By leveraging AI to present complex data in comprehensible, engaging formats, it has elevated the viewer experience to unprecedented levels. Fans now enjoy not just the thrill of the game, but also the intricate strategies and personal triumphs that make cricket the beloved sport it is. As AI technology continues to evolve, the scope and impact of visual analytics in cricket broadcasting will only expand, promising even more exciting innovations in the future.

Chapter 16:
The Economic Impact of AI in Cricket

Artificial intelligence is having a transformative impact on cricket, in ways that go beyond the boundary ropes. The technology has not only revolutionised player performance and strategic decision-making, but it has also significantly influenced the cricket economy. From enhancing fan engagement to driving revenue growth, AI's economic footprint in cricket is both extensive and compelling.

The economic considerations of implementing AI in cricket are multi-faceted. On one hand, the initial costs of AI integration can be substantial. Tools such as advanced data analytics platforms, AI-driven training exercises, and intelligent stadium infrastructure require considerable investment. On the other hand, the long-term financial benefits often outweigh these initial outlays. Clubs and cricket boards have found that AI helps optimise multiple facets of the game, leading to cost savings and new revenue channels.

One area where AI shows its economic muscle is in fan engagement. Cricket boards and franchises leverage AI to tailor the fan experience, both in-stadium and online. Personalised content delivered through AI algorithms can increase fan interaction and loyalty. For example, algorithms analyse fan behaviour to recommend match clips, interviews, and articles. Higher engagement often translates into increased merchandise sales, subscription revenues, and sponsorship deals.

Furthermore, AI's predictive analytics play a crucial role in ticket pricing strategies. By analysing historical data and current market trends, AI tools can help franchises set optimal ticket prices to maximise attendance and revenue. Dynamic pricing models adjust in real-time based on variables such as weather conditions, team performance, and even social media sentiment. This level of sophistication ensures that revenue from ticket sales is maximised while maintaining accessibility for fans.

Broadcasters, too, reap economic benefits from AI. Enhanced AI-driven commentary and visual analytics not only enrich the viewing experience but can also attract higher advertisement revenues. Broadcasters use AI to provide real-time statistics, player insights, and predictive analysis, offering an immersive experience for viewers. This leads to longer viewing times and, consequently, more advertising potential. The ability to customise advertisements based on viewer data further enhances revenue streams.

Moreover, AI is an invaluable tool for sponsorship valuation. Brands look for maximum return on investment when sponsoring teams or tournaments. AI enables more accurate measurement of a sponsorship's reach and impact, helping brands gauge the effectiveness of their investments. This accurate valuation can lead to better-negotiated deals, benefiting both the sponsor and the cricket body. By leveraging AI, brands can also engage in targeted marketing, using data analytics to reach the most relevant audience segments.

AI's economic impact extends to player recruitment and talent development. Historically, scouting talented players required extensive human labour and was often limited by geography. AI-driven systems can analyse and rank players based on performance metrics, providing a broader talent pool for teams to choose from. By identifying high-potential players early, franchises can secure talent more cost-effectively, reducing expenditure on high-profile signings. These savings can be reallocated to other areas, such as infrastructure and youth development programs.

Training and injury management systems powered by AI also contribute to economic efficiency. Predictive models can forecast injury risks, allowing teams to take preventative measures. This reduces medical expenses and ensures star players stay fit, maintaining their commercial value. Machine learning algorithms personalise training regimens, often reducing the time and resources required to achieve peak performance. The net result is a more efficient use of manpower and a reduction in operational costs.

Let's not overlook the role of AI in grassroots and amateur cricket. Traditionally, funding and resources for these levels of cricket have been limited. AI technology can democratise access to high-quality training tools and performance analytics, fostering talent development from the ground up. As talent from these levels progresses to professional cricket, the quality of the sport improves, which in turn attracts more sponsorship and media revenue.

Intelligent infrastructure, such as AI-powered stadiums, also brings substantial economic benefits. Smart stadiums enhance the fan experience with features like seamless ticketing, personalised concessions, and interactive entertainment. These enhancements can lead to increased attendance and higher per capita spending. AI systems also streamline stadium operations, from crowd control to energy management, reducing operational costs.

The integration of AI in cricket brings about substantial economies of scale, especially for large tournaments like the Cricket World Cup and T20 leagues. Efficiency in logistics, player management, and match scheduling can reduce costs substantially. For instance, AI-driven predictive models can optimise travel schedules and hotel bookings, leading to significant savings.

Overall, the economic impact of AI in cricket is multifaceted and far-reaching. It presents numerous opportunities for revenue generation, cost savings, and operational efficiency. As AI technology advances and becomes more accessible, these economic advantages are likely to become even more pronounced. The initial investment in AI may be substantial, but the return on investment makes it a compelling proposition for cricket boards, franchises, and other stakeholders in the sport.

The transformative potential of AI in cricket is undeniable. But just as importantly, it underscores a broader trend where sports increasingly rely on technology to enhance both performance and profitability. As other sports observe these benefits, it wouldn't be surprising to see a more widespread adoption of AI, shaping the economy of sports globally. By investing in AI, cricket positions itself at the forefront of this technological revolution, ensuring its economic viability and competitive edge for years to come.

Chapter 17:
Ethical Considerations in AI Usage

When cricket enthusiasts and analysts marvel at the integration of artificial intelligence in their beloved sport, they often overlook one critical aspect – ethics. Ethical considerations are essential in shaping how AI is leveraged within the realms of cricket. Without ethical guidelines, we may risk undermining the sport's integrity and the values it upholds.

Ethical considerations in AI usage span various dimensions, ranging from fairness and transparency to data privacy and the potential for creating biases. Let's start with the notion of fairness. At its core, cricket is a game that celebrates fair play. When AI systems are introduced, it's paramount that these systems themselves operate on principles of equity. For instance, any AI-driven decision-making tool should be devoid of biases that could unfairly advantage or disadvantage any player or team. But ensuring this requires meticulous scrutiny of the algorithms and data sets used in these AI systems.

Transparency is another pressing concern. AI in cricket isn't just about efficiency and getting results faster; it's also about trust. Players, coaches, and fans must be able to trust that the AI systems are making decisions based on clear, understandable criteria. If an AI system recommends a strategic move, there should be transparency regarding how that recommendation was derived. Lack of transparency breeds suspicion and can erode the very fabric of sportsmanship that cricket cherishes.

What about data privacy? AI relies heavily on data – player performance, physical health metrics, game statistics, and more. With so much data being collected and processed, safeguarding the privacy of individuals is imperative. Let's consider wearable technology used to monitor players' health and performance. While this data contributes significantly to enhancing performance and preventing injuries, it's crucial to ensure that such personal information is stored securely and used ethically. Players should have a say in how their data is utilised and who gets access to it.

Moreover, the issue of consent cannot be ignored. Players should be informed and should consent to the collection and use of their data. This isn't just about ticking a box; it's about genuinely understanding what data will be collected and how it will be used. In a sport where camaraderie and trust play vital roles, obtaining genuine consent is non-negotiable.

Also, ethical considerations must address the creation and reinforcement of biases. Even seemingly objective data can harbour inherent biases, whether they are based on geographical location, past performance trends, or unconscious biases encoded by developers. AI systems developed without a keen eye for bias mitigation can perpetuate or even exacerbate these biases. For instance, if a scouting tool disproportionately favours players from certain regions due to historical performance data, it may overlook emerging talent from less renowned areas. Hence, continuous auditing of AI systems for biases is necessary to preserve the inclusiveness and fairness the sport aims to promote.

Then, there's the matter of the human element in cricket. AI technologies promise several enhancements, from performance metrics to strategic recommendations, yet they should not replace human judgment entirely. Cricket is not merely a game of numbers and probabilities; it's about intuition, experience, and sometimes, even gut feeling. A balance must be struck where AI supports and augments human decision-making rather than replacing it. The human element should remain central, with AI serving as a complementary tool rather than a crutch.

Furthermore, the accessibility of AI technologies raises another ethical quandary. High-tech AI solutions often come with significant costs. Wealthier teams and cricket boards may afford cutting-edge AI tools, creating a disparity between them and financially weaker teams. Such imbalances can exacerbate existing inequalities in the sport. Efforts should be made to democratise access to AI technologies, ensuring that all teams, regardless of their financial stature, benefit equally from AI advancements.

Let's also talk about the implications for the workforce within cricket. With AI taking over certain analytical and operational roles, there might be concerns about job displacement. Analysts, scouts, and even coaching staff might find their roles evolving or, in worst-case scenarios, becoming redundant. While technology brings efficiencies, the transition should be managed with empathy and foresight, offering retraining and upskilling opportunities to affected professionals.

Finally, the broader societal impact cannot be undermined. Cricket isn't just a sport; it's a cultural phenomenon that impacts societies worldwide. The ethical deployment of AI in cricket can set a precedent for other sports and sectors. It's a stewardship that cricket must handle with caution and responsibility, reflecting the highest standards of ethical practice.

In summary, the transformative potential of AI in cricket is undeniable. However, its ultimate success hinges on addressing ethical considerations rigorously. Fairness, transparency, data privacy, consent, bias mitigation, maintaining the human element, accessibility, workforce implications, and societal impact – these are the pillars upon which the ethical foundation of AI in cricket must rest. By vigilantly upholding these ethics, cricket can harness AI's power while preserving the spirit and values intrinsic to the game.

As we move forward, it is essential for all stakeholders – players, coaches, administrators, fans, and technologists – to engage in ongoing dialogue about these ethical considerations. The goal is not just to leverage AI for its benefits but to do so in a manner that upholds and enhances the integrity of the sport. Only then can we genuinely say that AI has found its rightful place in the world of cricket, augmenting its beauty, fairness, and competitive spirit.

The road ahead is promising yet fraught with challenges. As cricket continues to evolve with AI, the lessons learnt here will undoubtedly resonate beyond the boundaries of the sport. By addressing ethical considerations today, we're not just shaping the future of cricket; we're setting standards for AI's role in our world tomorrow.

Chapter 18:
Case Studies of AI Implementation

Delving into the practical realm, this chapter brings forth compelling case studies that highlight the transformative impact of AI in cricket. Take, for instance, the deployment of AI by national teams like England, who now utilise machine learning algorithms to fine-tune their players' techniques based on historical data and real-time performance metrics. Another striking example is the IPL franchises leveraging predictive analytics to scout talent more efficiently, thereby ensuring they assemble competitive teams season after season. These instances underscore not only the successful integration of AI solutions but also unveil invaluable lessons for future innovations and refinements. With each case study, we see a vivid portrayal of AI's ability to elevate the game, making cricket not just a sport of passion, but also one of precision and strategy. As we explore these exemplars, the overarching narrative remains clear: artificial intelligence is revolutionising cricket in ways once thought impossible.

Successful Examples

The implementation of artificial intelligence in cricket has led to transformative changes across various facets of the game. These successful instances underscore AI's capacity to revolutionise cricketer performance, strategic planning, and the overarching experience for both players and fans.

One of the most striking examples of AI's impact is in data-driven player analysis. International cricket teams, such as the Indian and Australian squads, have leveraged AI to delve deeper into player performance metrics. By analysing a plethora of data points, ranging from ball trajectory to bat angles, teams can pinpoint areas for improvement with unparalleled accuracy. This meticulous analysis not only assists in refining player techniques but also in tailoring training regimens to optimise individual strengths and weaknesses.

Injury prevention and management have also seen significant advancements, particularly with wearable technology combined with predictive modelling. The England Cricket Board (ECB) incorporated AI-driven wearables that monitor players' physiological and biomechanical data. These wearables can predict the likelihood of injuries and suggest preventive measures. For instance, during the Ashes series, real-time data from these devices helped the English team make early interventions, ensuring their key players remained fit and competitive throughout the tournament.

AI's influence extends beyond player fitness and into tactical realms. On-field strategy, for instance, has been transformed by machine learning algorithms that process historical and real-time match data to suggest optimal field placements and batting orders. The collaboration between Cricket Australia and data analytics firms resulted in an AI system that could simulate various match scenarios. This tool proved invaluable during the 2015 World Cup, where dynamic on-field adjustments, guided by predictive analytics, played a pivotal role in Australia's triumph.

Changing gears to player scouting and recruitment, AI has made significant strides in identifying emerging talent. IPL teams like the Mumbai Indians and Chennai Super Kings utilise AI algorithms to scrutinize player performances across domestic leagues, pinpointing promising cricketers who might otherwise fly under the radar. The IPL

2020 auction saw several players being recruited based on AI-driven insights, which factored in not only their past performances but also their potential future development.

Focusing on opponent analysis and strategy formulation, AI has become a game-changer. Teams like New Zealand and South Africa use AI to dissect opponents' playing patterns and strategise accordingly. In the 2019 ICC Cricket World Cup, New Zealand's remarkable journey to the final was, in part, attributed to their use of AI for opponent analysis. By comprehensively understanding opponents' strategies and movements, they were able to devise game plans that rendered traditional strengths ineffective.

Big data integration has become the backbone of modern-day cricket strategy. Overwhelming volumes of data accrued from matches, player performances, and even fan interactions are processed using sophisticated AI tools. Teams such as Pakistan's national team have embraced this data-centric approach, leveraging AI to enhance their analytics capabilities. The result is an intricate understanding of the game, allowing for refinements that marginally elevate overall performance but cumulatively make significant impacts.

The umpiring and Decision Review System (DRS) have also benefitted greatly from AI-enhanced accuracy. Hawk-Eye technology, an integral part of DRS, uses AI to track ball trajectories and enable precise decision-making. During the 2020 ICC T20 World Cup, AI-driven DRS minimised human error and ensured that contentious decisions were reviewed with scientific precision, adding a layer of fairness and reliability to the sport.

AI has played a pivotal role in enhancing fan engagement as well. Platforms powered by AI provide personalised content, tailor-made to fans' preferences. The Indian Premier League (IPL) has successfully integrated AI to enhance the viewing experience. Their AI-driven analyses offer insights into match strategies and player performances, engaging fans on a deeper, more interactive level. This enrichment of content not only attracts a broader audience but also sustains their interest, leading to higher viewership and fan loyalty.

Through virtual and augmented reality, AI has brought fans closer to the action than ever before. Cricket simulations and VR experiences, driven by AI, offer immersive views and interactive elements that transform passive watching into active participation. The West Indies Cricket Board has pioneered several initiatives that utilise VR and AR, giving fans the virtual sensation of being on the field. This blend of AI technologies revolutionises the fan experience, creating an engaging and memorable connection to the sport.

In cricket broadcasting, AI is proving to be a formidable ally. AI-powered commentary provides real-time, insightful analyses that enhance viewers' understanding of the game. For example, during live broadcasts of the Big Bash League (BBL), AI systems analyse on-field actions and deliver in-depth statistics and performance metrics, complementing the commentators' narratives. Visual analytics backed by AI have similarly transformed match graphics, offering detailed and dynamic representations of player positioning, scoring patterns, and much more.

Economic impacts of AI in cricket cannot be overstated. Franchises and cricket boards are witnessing significant returns on investments made in AI, from bolstering player performances to augmenting fan engagement and, incrementally, boosting revenues. The financial success following AI implementation in leagues like the IPL and BBL sets a precedent for other cricketing bodies to follow, proving that AI is not merely a technological enhancement but a potent economic lever.

However, the true power of AI in cricket also lies in its potential to drive the sport forward. With ongoing advancements, there's a collective push towards smarter, data-driven cricket. These successful examples are just the beginning, setting a foundation for an AI-integrated future where cricket evolves to new, exciting heights. The potential for AI to revolutionise the sport—even further than it already has—is immense and continues to inspire players, coaches, analysts, and fans alike to reimagine what's possible within the realm of cricket.

In conclusion, AI implementations have yielded transformative outcomes across the cricketing spectrum. Whether it's enhancing player performance, optimising strategies, or revolutionising the fan experience, these successful examples punctuate the burgeoning relationship between cricket and artificial intelligence. As this relationship deepens, we can only anticipate more innovative breakthroughs that will redefine how we play, watch, and understand this beloved sport.

Lessons Learned

Reflecting on the case studies of AI implementation in cricket reveals crucial insights that extend beyond the boundaries of the sport itself. A recurring theme is the transformative power of AI to not only enhance performance and decision-making but also to fundamentally alter the entire ecosystem surrounding the game. These lessons underscore the immense potential and the challenges inherent in integrating cutting-edge technology with a century-old sport.

One of the most significant lessons is the importance of data quality and its accessibility. The success of AI in cricket, as demonstrated in various implementations, hinges on the availability of high-fidelity data. Poor data quality can lead to inaccurate predictions and ineffective strategies, which could undermine the trust in AI systems. Ensuring comprehensive and accurate data collection mechanisms is paramount, necessitating robust data governance frameworks that go hand-in-hand with AI adoption.

Another key lesson is the necessity of a symbiotic relationship between human expertise and AI capabilities. The case studies illustrate that, while AI can process vast amounts of data far quicker than any human can, the interpretative skills and intuitive insights of human experts are irreplaceable. The triumphs of AI in cricket often come when the technology is used as a tool to augment human decision-making, rather than replace it. This collaborative approach fosters an environment where technology and human intellect coalesce to achieve superior outcomes.

Moreover, adaptation and continuous learning are critical components in the effective implementation of AI in cricket. The dynamic nature of sports means that models and algorithms need regular updates to stay relevant and accurate. The case studies repeatedly emphasise the need for an iterative approach to AI development, involving frequent testing, validation, and refinement based on real-world performance and feedback. This cyclical process embodies the very principles of machine learning, reinforcing the concept of perpetual improvement.

Equally essential is the cultural shift within organisations to embrace AI-driven strategies. The introduction of any disruptive technology often meets with resistance, and AI is no exception. The case examples highlight that educational initiatives play a vital role in easing this transition. Training programmes and workshops can demystify AI, helping players, coaches, and administrative staff to understand and trust the technology. Bridging the knowledge gap and addressing apprehensions directly contribute to smoother, more effective AI integration.

The significance of ethical considerations and fairness in AI applications cannot be overstated. Case studies shed light on the ethical dilemmas that arise when deploying AI, such as biases in data sets that could yield unfair advantages or discriminate unintentionally. Establishing ethical guidelines and ensuring transparency in AI processes are crucial steps in fostering trust and fairness. An ethical approach not only builds credibility but also promotes the broader acceptance of AI technologies.

Scalability and customisation stand out as critical factors influencing the impact of AI in cricket. The ability to tailor AI solutions to meet specific needs, whether for individual player performance, team strategies, or fan engagement, enhances their effectiveness. Furthermore, scalable solutions that can be adapted across different levels of the game—from grassroots to professional tiers—illustrate the versatility and far-reaching benefits of AI. These characteristics will likely dictate the future landscape of AI in cricket, where bespoke solutions cater to diverse requirements.

Perhaps one of the most inspirational lessons learned is the role of AI in democratising cricket. By providing access to advanced analytics and performance metrics, AI levels the playing field, empowering emerging players and smaller teams to compete more effectively with established giants. This shift towards inclusivity can galvanise the sport, uncovering hidden talents and fostering a more competitive and thrilling environment for all stakeholders involved.

The application of AI in injury prevention and management, as reflected in the case studies, also offers profound learnings. AI technologies, particularly those employing wearables and predictive modelling, have shown remarkable promise in reducing injury risks. This not only safeguards players' careers but also has long-term implications for their health and well-being. The predictive nature of AI provides preemptive solutions, underscoring the preventative potential rather than merely reactive measures. This proactive stance can revolutionise how teams approach player welfare, marking a paradigm shift in sports medicine within cricket.

Furthermore, the anecdotal successes in AI-enhanced strategy formulation and in-game decision-making highlight the profound influence of technology on strategic evolution. The agility and precision that AI brings to real-time decisions illustrate how deeply it can augment traditional methodologies. By offering insights that were previously unattainable, AI reshapes strategic paradigms, pushing the boundaries of what is considered possible in cricket management.

On a practical level, the economic ramifications of AI implementation are also worth noting. While the initial investment may be substantial, the long-term cost savings and revenue potential are significant. Case studies illustrate that AI's ability to optimise performance and enhance fan engagement translates into tangible financial benefits. These economic incentives can drive further investment and innovation in AI, creating a virtuous cycle of growth and advancement.

In conclusion, the lessons learned from the case studies of AI implementation in cricket are multifaceted, reflecting both the opportunities and challenges that come with technological integration. They underscore the necessity of high-quality data, the synergy between human and machine intelligence, the importance of iterative learning, and the need for organisational cultural shifts. Ethical considerations, scalability, and economic impacts also play crucial roles in shaping the AI landscape. By embracing these lessons, the cricket community can harness AI's full potential, ushering in a new era of evolution and excellence in the sport.

Chapter 19:
The Future of Training and Talent Development

The world of cricket is on the brink of transformative change, driven primarily by advancements in artificial intelligence. As we look forward to the future of training and talent development, we see a landscape rich with potential. AI is not just a tool for data analytics but is set to revolutionise every facet of how players train, develop their skills, and even how teams scout for new talent. The implications are vast, stretching from grassroots cricket to the professional level.

AI's integration into training regimens promises not only precision but also personalised experiences for athletes. Imagine a budding cricketer receiving coaching customised to their unique strengths and weaknesses, all made possible through AI. This isn't a distant fantasy; it's becoming a reality. Machine learning algorithms can analyse hundreds of hours of gameplay, identifying areas for improvement and tailoring exercises to address these gaps. Such bespoke training programs can expedite the development of talent, ensuring that players reach their full potential much faster.

Consider the traditional methods of training where coaches rely on their experience and instinct to guide players. While invaluable, these methods can be subjective. AI offers an objective layer of analysis, combining vast datasets to identify subtle patterns and trends that a human eye might miss. This objective approach ensures that no aspect of a player's game is neglected, fostering more rounded cricketers. For instance, AI can pinpoint the minute shifts in a bowler's action that could lead to injuries, thereby preventing them before they occur.

Moreover, AI-driven performance analytics are already making waves. Players can now access in-depth reports that detail every nuance of their performance. From the angle of their wrist during a delivery to the foot placement while batting, these insights are invaluable. With real-time feedback, cricketers can adjust their techniques on the fly, honing their skills with every practice session.

Another fascinating frontier is the use of virtual and augmented reality in training. With VR, players can simulate match conditions, practice against different types of bowlers, and make strategic decisions in real-time, all within a controlled environment. Augmented reality can overlay data onto the physical world, allowing players to visualise ball trajectories, optimal foot placements, and more. These technologies are set to make training sessions more immersive and effective, offering experiences that were once impossible.

Scouting for new talent is another area ripe for transformation. Traditionally, scouts would travel far and wide, observing countless matches to identify promising players. This method, while tried and true, is far from efficient. With AI, the process can be streamlined and enhanced. By analysing vast datasets from matches across the globe, AI can identify emerging talents who might have otherwise gone unnoticed. Algorithms can evaluate a player's performance metrics, growth potential, and even psychological robustness, ensuring that scouts focus their attention on candidates with the highest potential for success.

Consider a young cricketer from a remote village, whose games are rarely watched by professional scouts. With AI, every performance can be recorded, analysed, and compared against global standards. This democratises the scouting process, giving opportunities to talents irrespective of their geographical location. It's a shift towards a more inclusive and merit-based system, ensuring that the best talents are discovered and nurtured.

Coaching, too, stands to benefit enormously. AI can assist coaches by providing them with detailed analytics, enabling them to develop more effective strategies and training plans. Coaches can track a player's progress over time, adjusting training regimens to address specific needs. The amalgamation of a coach's instinct and experience with AI's analytical prowess can create a formidable partnership, pushing the boundaries of what is possible in player development.

Additionally, the psychological aspect of training is gaining more recognition. Modern cricket is as much a mental game as it is a physical one. AI can help in monitoring a player's psychological wellbeing, offering insights into their mental state and suggesting interventions when necessary. For example, AI tools can analyse a player's body language, speech patterns, and social interactions to gauge stress levels, providing early warnings and allowing for timely support.

The implications extend beyond individual players. Teams can use AI to develop cohesive training plans that optimise the collective performance. By analysing how players perform together, coaches can devise strategies that play to the team's strengths and mitigate weaknesses. This holistic approach ensures that teams are well-prepared, adaptable, and resilient in the face of competition.

AI is also poised to influence the way recovery and rehabilitation are approached. With predictive modelling, injuries can be anticipated and managed more effectively. Players can follow rehab programs that are tailored specifically to their conditions, reducing recovery times and preventing re-injuries. This ensures that players are not just physically fit but also mentally ready to get back into the game.

Another fascinating development is the potential for AI to aid in tactical training. Interactive AI programs can simulate different game scenarios, allowing players to practice and strategise in a virtual environment. This not only sharpens their tactical acumen but also helps them remain composed under pressure. By rehearsing strategies in a controlled setting, players can perform more effectively during actual matches.

What does all this mean for the future of cricket? The sport is set to become more competitive, with a higher overall standard of play. Players will be better prepared, more skilled, and more strategically savvy. This raises the bar, not just for individual performance but for the sport as a whole. Spectators, too, will benefit, enjoying games that are more exciting and closely contested.

In conclusion, the future of training and talent development in cricket is brighter than ever. AI promises to bring precision, personalisation, and efficiency to every aspect of player development. As these technologies continue to evolve, they will unlock new possibilities, making the game more inclusive and competitive. Coaches, players, and teams that embrace these advancements will lead the way, redefining the standards of excellence in cricket.

As we look ahead, one thing is clear: the fusion of AI and cricket is not just a fleeting trend but a transformative force that will shape the future of the sport. The changes we are witnessing are just the beginning, promising a future where talent is nurtured like never before and the game of cricket reaches unprecedented heights.

Chapter 20:
AI's Role in Women's Cricket

Women's cricket has experienced a transformative evolution over the past decade. With increasing global viewership and investment, this dynamic sport has gained a well-deserved spotlight. Central to this evolution is the incorporation of Artificial Intelligence (AI), which has begun to influence every facet of the game. From training regimes to match strategies, and even fan engagement, AI is reshaping women's cricket in profound ways.

One of the most striking impacts of AI in women's cricket lies in player performance and development. Historically, the analysis of player performances has been somewhat subjective, relying heavily on the expertise of coaches and analysts. Now, with AI, data-driven insights provide a more granular understanding of a player's strengths and areas for improvement. Sophisticated algorithms assess a multitude of variables like batting angles, bowling speeds, and even reaction times, offering tailored training programs that help players achieve peak performance.

The infusion of AI isn't confined to individual player development. It also enhances team dynamics. AI systems analyse vast amounts of data from previous matches, identifying patterns and suggesting optimal combinations for team line-ups. For instance, by studying a bowler's history against a particular batter, AI can forecast the most effective bowling strategy. This level of detailed analysis was once unthinkable, but it's now becoming indispensable for teams aiming for competitive edge.

Another significant area where AI contributes to women's cricket is in the realm of injury prevention and management. Female athletes often face unique physiological challenges that differ from their male counterparts. AI leverages wearable technology to monitor vital parameters in real-time, predicting potential injuries before they occur. Through predictive modelling, patterns in data can warn coaching staff of high-risk scenarios, allowing for timely interventions and modified training regimes to ensure players stay fit and healthy.

The implementation of AI has also revolutionised how coaches interact with their players. AI-driven insights are invaluable in providing objective feedback. During training sessions, intelligent systems can track a player's movements and provide instant feedback on technique. For instance, if a bowler's arm position deviates from the optimal angle, the system flags this anomaly, helping the player to correct it immediately. This real-time feedback loop ensures continuous improvement and accelerates skill acquisition.

Real-time match-day adjustments represent another frontier for AI in women's cricket. When every decision can change the course of the game, having AI as a strategic asset becomes invaluable. AI interprets on-field data, providing real-time recommendations on adjustments in field placements, batting orders, or bowling changes. These recommendations, backed by immense datasets, empower captains and coaches to make informed decisions under pressure, thereby enhancing the overall competitive standard of women's cricket.

AI's influence reaches beyond the boundary lines, extending into player scouting and recruitment. The traditional scouting process, often restricted by geographical and logistical limitations, has been transformed. AI systems can evaluate a players' potential by analysing video footage and performance data from various leagues and tournaments across the world. This opens up opportunities for discovering untapped talent in remote regions, ensuring that promising female cricketers have the platform to showcase their skills on the global stage.

Moreover, AI is redefining how teams prepare for their opponents. Through detailed analysis of opponents' strengths, weaknesses, and tendencies, AI generates comprehensive dossiers that inform prematch strategy sessions. This level of preparation allows teams to devise bespoke game plans tailored to counter specific threats, giving them a strategic advantage and elevating the complexity and calibre of women's cricket competitions.

When it comes to enhancing the fan experience, AI is equally transformative. Today's fans demand personalisation and engagement, and AI delivers just that. By analysing viewer data, AI helps curate personalised content and immersive viewing experiences. Features such as AI-powered commentary, real-time statistics, and predictive scores make the game more engaging, catering to the evolving demands of the modern cricket fan.

In the broadcasting domain, AI-driven visual analytics provide richer storytelling. Enhanced graphics, heat maps, and predictive models inform the audience, bringing them closer to the nuances of the game. For women's cricket, which is gaining a larger global following, this elevated broadcasting standard ensures that the sport is presented with the professionalism and flair it deserves.

The integration of AI in women's cricket also brings about significant economic implications. Higher accuracy in performance analytics and injury prevention can translate into prolonged careers for players. This not only increases the players' earning potential but also ensures a sustained pool of talent, contributing to the sport's overall growth. Furthermore, the ability to discover and develop new talent efficiently means franchises and national teams can invest wisely, maximising returns and fostering a sustainable ecosystem for women's cricket.

However, the ethical considerations of AI in women's cricket can't be overlooked. While AI brings numerous advantages, it's crucial to address issues related to data privacy and the potential for over-reliance on technology. Ensuring transparent and equitable use of AI remains a collective responsibility for all stakeholders in the cricketing community. Maintaining a balance where AI aids human judgment without overtaking it is necessary for the long-term integrity of the sport.

In conclusion, AI's role in women's cricket is nothing short of revolutionary. From honing individual skills to enhancing team strategies and boosting fan engagement, the potential of AI is immense. As the sport continues to grow, integrating AI in a balanced and ethical manner will be key to unlocking the full potential of women's cricket. The marriage of technology and talent offers an exciting future, ensuring that the sport not only evolves but continues to captivate audiences worldwide.

AI is more than a tool; it's a catalyst for the next era of women's cricket, promising a future where performance and passion seamlessly intertwine, making every game a spectacle of skill, strategy, and dedication.

Chapter 21:
AI in Grassroots and Amateur Cricket

Cricket isn't just about the big stadiums and international matches. At its heart, the sport thrives in local parks, club grounds, and school fields. It's in these grassroots and amateur settings that the real passion for the game is ignited. But even here, artificial intelligence (AI) is beginning to make its presence felt. The technology that once seemed exclusive to professional arenas is now seeping into the grassroots level, transforming how the game is played and experienced.

At the grassroots level, AI's impact is profoundly shaping talent recognition. Traditional talent identification processes can be somewhat subjective, heavily reliant on the eyes and opinions of seasoned coaches. However, AI-powered analytics platforms are providing a more objective lens. These tools can assess players' performances by analysing video footage and extracting performance metrics. This data-driven approach helps in distinguishing genuine talent from mere flashes of brilliance.

Moreover, AI has democratised access to high-quality coaching. Not every amateur player has the luxury of professional coaching. AI-driven coaching apps fill this gap by offering personalised training plans and feedback. For instance, an app can track a bowler's arm motion and suggest adjustments in real-time, similar to what a live coach would do. This means that players, regardless of their geographical or financial limitations, can now polish their skills with high-level insights.

Statistics and data analytics are no longer the exclusive domain of professional teams. Even local cricket clubs are starting to leverage AI to analyse games and players. Apps and software platforms can break down a player's innings or a bowler's spell into minute details. Information about shot selection, foot movement, and even the angle of the bat during impact is all readily available. With such rich data, team strategies can be fine-tuned to exploit opponents' weaknesses and enhance one's strengths.

Accessibility to video analysis tools has brought a new dimension to grassroots cricket. Simple setups involving a smartphone and a tripod can capture detailed footage of matches and training sessions. AI algorithms can then dissect these videos to provide feedback on batting techniques, bowling actions, and field placements. What was once a luxury only accessible to elite sports academies is now available to weekend warriors and school teams alike.

Preparation for matches has also evolved. AI tools can simulate game scenarios based on the collected data, helping players to mentally prepare for various situations. If a batsman tends to struggle against left-arm spinners, the AI can simulate multiple deliveries that replicate challenges posed by such bowlers. This way, practice isn't just random but is geared towards overcoming specific weaknesses.

Injury prevention is another critical area where AI is making significant strides at the amateur level. Wearable devices, combined with predictive modelling, can monitor physical stress and fatigue levels. They can alert a player when they are at risk of injury, suggesting rest or modified training to prevent long-term damage. This is especially beneficial for young, aspiring cricketers who often overlook the importance of managing their physical workload.

AI has also brought about advancements in game administration and management. Managing a local league involves various tasks, from scheduling matches to keeping track of player stats. AI-driven platforms streamline these processes, making administration more efficient. Automated scheduling, digital scorecards, and performance tracking save time and reduce the chances of human error.

Community engagement benefits as well. Club websites and apps powered by AI can offer customised content for fans and members, including match highlights, player profiles, and personalised newsletters. This level of engagement, previously seen only in professional set-ups, helps build a strong, connected community at the grassroots level.

The role of AI in grassroots cricket isn't just limited to players and teams; it's also reshaping the experience for amateur match officials. AI tools for umpires can assist in decision-making processes, helping even the smallest clubs to ensure fair play. Technologies akin to the Decision Review System (DRS) used in international matches can now be accessed at a fraction of the cost. This makes umpiring more accurate and reduces disputes, fostering a spirit of fair competition.

AI's capacity to learn and adapt means these systems get better over time. As more data is collected and analysed, recommendations, predictions, and strategies become increasingly refined. This continuous improvement loop ensures that grassroots players and teams can benefit from cutting-edge insights year after year.

Indeed, the impact of AI at the grassroots level goes beyond individual performance and match outcomes. It has the potential to democratise the game of cricket, making high-quality coaching, strategy, and analysis accessible to anyone with a love for the sport. This could lead to a more level playing field where talent, irrespective of one's background, gets the chance to shine.

The motivational boost that AI provides cannot be overstated. The ability to track progress through precise data analytics can be incredibly encouraging for amateur players. Seeing measurable improvements in their game based on factual data builds confidence and keeps the passion alive. It's this empowerment that can propel a hobbyist to pursue cricket more seriously, possibly even making the leap to professional levels.

The ripple effect of these advancements will likely see an elevation in the overall standard of amateur cricket. As more players start adopting these technologies, the quality of competition rises, which in turn feeds back into the system, pushing everyone to up their game. This virtuous cycle of improvement fosters an environment where excellence becomes the norm rather than the exception.

AI is not a silver bullet; challenges and limitations exist. Access remains uneven, primarily due to the cost factor and varying levels of tech-savviness. Resistance to change is another hurdle, with traditionalists sometimes wary of the algorithms taking over age-old coaching methods. Yet, the inexorable march of technology suggests that these are but temporary setbacks.

In conclusion, artificial intelligence is revolutionising grassroots and amateur cricket in ways that were unimaginable a few years ago. From talent identification and personalised coaching to injury prevention and community engagement, the influence of AI is profound and far-reaching. It's a brave new world for cricket enthusiasts at every level, and the game is richer for it.

Chapter 22:
Building Smarter Stadiums

As we dive into the realm of smarter stadiums, it's clear that the heart of cricket is evolving beyond the pitch. Modern stadiums are morphing into intelligent coliseums, leveraging artificial intelligence to enhance every facet of a cricket match. From automated traffic management systems and smart parking solutions that ease the journey to the venue, to real-time crowd monitoring ensuring safety and efficient resource management, the infrastructure itself is becoming more intuitive. Fans aren't just passive spectators anymore; they interact dynamically through AI-driven personalised experiences—imagine getting instant match statistics, food and beverage updates, and even fan polls directly to their smart devices. Ground maintenance too, has seen a revolution with sensors and machine learning ensuring optimal pitch conditions. These advancements are shaping not just the stadiums, but transforming every match into a seamlessly orchestrated experience, breathing new life into the tradition-rich sport of cricket.

Intelligent Infrastructure

Imagine stepping into a cricket stadium that feels alive. The pitch beneath your feet isn't just grass; it's equipped with sensors that transmit real-time data about moisture levels, wear and tear, and temperature variations. The stands are filled with fans, each engaged in their personalised game experience, thanks to an interconnected technological ecosystem. This is not a distant vision but the unfolding reality of intelligent infrastructure within smarter stadiums.

The core of intelligent infrastructure revolves around integrating advanced technologies into the physical fabric of cricket venues. These technologies harness the power of AI, IoT (Internet of Things), and big data analytics to create an environment that is not just reactive but also proactive. From optimising match-day operations to improving the fan experience, the applications are as varied as they are profound.

Starting with the playing field itself, AI-driven irrigation systems and ground conditions monitoring help maintain optimal conditions. Automated sensors embedded in the soil gather data on moisture, temperature, and grass health. Groundstaff can access this data in real-time, allowing for more precise and efficient maintenance practices. This integration ensures that the pitch remains in perfect condition, irrespective of the climatic challenges that it may face.

Beyond the pitch, consider the stands where spectators are seated. Equipped with IoT sensors, these seats adapt to weather conditions, offering warming or cooling functionalities to enhance comfort. These same sensors collect data on crowd density and movement, empowering stadium management to make real-time decisions to alleviate congestion and ensure safety. Smart seating can also localise promotional offers and live feeds, tailoring the experience to each fan's preferences and increasing engagement.

Effective crowd management is integral to intelligent infrastructure. AI-driven surveillance systems monitor entry and exit points, providing real-time updates on crowd flow. These systems can identify bottlenecks and suggest alternative routes, ensuring swift and orderly movement of people. Furthermore, intelligent infrastructure allows for a more robust security apparatus, identifying potential threats before they escalate and deploying resources intelligently to address them.

Moreover, intelligent infrastructure extends to sustainability efforts. AI can optimise energy consumption throughout the stadium, from lighting and HVAC systems to power management in concession stands. Smart grids and renewable energy sources like solar panels work in harmony, cutting down on the venue's carbon footprint. Smart waste management systems segregate recyclables and compostables effectively, promoting eco-friendly practices among attendees.

Integration extends to the logistical elements of a match day. AI can streamline transport systems around the stadium, predicting traffic patterns and providing real-time updates to fans and transit authorities. On match days, this means using AI algorithms that process historical and real-time data to optimize bus and train schedules, reducing delays and ensuring a smooth flow of spectators to and from the ground.

But intelligent infrastructure isn't confined to operational efficiencies; it also revolutionises the fan experience. Personalisation driven by AI ensures that each attendee receives content tailored to their interests, from customised game statistics to targeted promotions. Fans can use their smartphones to interact with smart kiosks that offer personalised refreshments based on their purchase history and dietary preferences. Enhanced connectivity ensures that these interactions are seamless, providing a user experience that is as comfortable as it is cutting-edge.

Interactive fan zones, bolstered by AR and VR technologies, allow spectators to engage with the game in entirely new ways. Smart screens provide AR overlays that deliver real-time statistics and player biographies as the match unfolds. These innovations create a dynamic, multi-dimensional viewing experience that extends beyond merely watching the game to becoming an integral part of the action.

Inclusivity also benefits from intelligent infrastructure. Accessibility features powered by AI can assist differently-abled fans, providing services like real-time captions, audio descriptions, and navigation assistance around the stadium. This ensures a more inclusive environment where everyone can enjoy the match-day experience to its fullest.

Lastly, intelligent infrastructure offers invaluable benefits to broadcasters and media. With smart cameras and robust data feeds, broadcasters can capture unique angles and deliver innovative visual analytics that enrich the viewer experience at home. Media zones equipped with high-speed data access ensure that journalists can report in real-time, bringing the latest updates to fans worldwide with unprecedented speed and detail.

The implementation of intelligent infrastructure in cricket stadiums truly embodies the spirit of AI's transformative potential. It facilitates operational efficiency, enhances fan engagement, and promotes sustainability, making cricket venues not just smarter but also more responsive and inclusive. As the sport continues to evolve, so too will the environments that host it, setting new standards for what a cricket stadium can be.

Fan Experience

The hallmark of modern sports isn't just the game itself but the holistic experience that wraps around it. Building smarter stadiums bridges a thrilling gap, where technology and the human penchant for emotional engagement intersect. To elevate the fan experience, AI-powered technologies have emerged as game-changers, creating an environment that is both interactive and immersive.

Entering a smart stadium today feels akin to stepping into the future. Imagine the turnstiles: they're no longer just a means to control entry but a point where fan engagement begins. AI technologies, combined with facial recognition, speed up entry procedures, reducing queues and minimising wait times. Fans are swiftly ushered in, having their excitement preserved rather than diminished by long lines.

Once inside, AI elevates the spectators' journey, making it more personalised and engaging. Through mobile apps integrated with AI, fans can access real-time data about the ongoing match, player statistics, and even historical data. These apps enhance the fan's knowledge and enjoyment of the game, turning a casual spectator into an informed aficionado.

Moreover, AI is revolutionising how fans navigate stadiums. Beacons and AI-driven wayfinding systems offer real-time guidance, helping fans locate amenities such as restrooms, food stalls, and their seats with ease. This integration ensures that even in large, sprawling stadiums, fans can move seamlessly, maintaining their focus on the game rather than the logistics of getting around.

The concession stands themselves have not been left untouched by this wave of innovation. AI-powered kiosks reduce wait times significantly. By predicting demand and managing inventory in real-time, these smart systems ensure that your favourite snack is always available when you want it. Additionally, with cashless payments and mobile ordering, fans no longer have to miss crucial moments waiting in line for food or beverages.

AI's role in enhancing the audiovisual experience in stadiums cannot be underplayed. Intelligent sound systems adjust acoustics automatically based on the stadium's occupancy and the nature of the event. Likewise, AI-enhanced lighting systems can alter in sync with the buzz of the game, creating electric atmospheres that heighten the excitement.

Consider the immense screens and display boards that have traditionally been used for showing scores. Now, enhanced with AI, these screens offer real-time analytics, deep dives into player performance, predictive outcomes, and can even highlight fan reactions. This interactive visual element keeps fans engaged and offers them a rich, layered understanding of the game as it unfolds.

Fan engagement extends beyond the stands into the realm of virtual and augmented reality. AI-driven VR and AR experiences can transport fans from anywhere in the world into the cricket stadium. Virtual seats offer an unparalleled, immersive view of the game, allowing fans to feel the thrill of being there, no matter where they are physically situated.

On the social front, AI analyses social media trends and fan interactions during live matches. This real-time analysis can drive unique fan experiences, such as showcasing fan tweets on big screens or offering exclusive content to those actively engaging online. It creates a community where fans feel valued and connected.

Personalised merchandising is another avenue AI has disrupted positively. Smart algorithms track fan preferences and suggest merchandise tailored to individual tastes. Whether it's a jersey with customised insignia or a memorabilia item linked to a memorable match, fans get to choose from curated options that resonate with their unique supporter journey.

Even the way fans relive memories has seen a transformation. AI technology curates personalised highlight packages that fans can watch post-match. These can focus specifically on the sequences and players they're most interested in, ensuring they never miss the moments that matter to them.

Smart stadiums also ensure fans' safety through AI-driven surveillance systems. These systems monitor crowd movements in real-time to detect unruly behaviour or potential hazards, enabling swift intervention. This application of AI not only makes the stadium experience more enjoyable but also provides peace of mind.

AI also fosters inclusivity. Customised solutions cater to fans with disabilities, offering them accessible seating, navigation assistance, and even descriptive commentary for visually impaired fans. This inclusivity ensures that the thrill of live sports is accessible to everyone, enhancing the community spirit of the game.

With all these advancements, the stadium experience transcends the mere act of watching cricket. It transforms into an interactive saga where each fan becomes an integral part of the narrative. In essence, AI doesn't replace the human element but enriches and amplifies it, creating a symphony where technology and human emotions harmonise beautifully.

As the AI-driven enhancements continue to evolve, the traditional barriers between fans and the game will keep diminishing. The result is a more connected, engaging, and seamless experience that respects the passion fans bring to cricket while offering them novel ways to express and deepen that passion. This is not merely an evolution; it is a revolution in how the beautiful game of cricket is experienced by its most dedicated followers.

Chapter 23:
Real-Time Strategy Games
Within Cricket

Cricket, often dubbed a gentleman's game, has evolved dramatically in strategy and execution. With artificial intelligence (AI) stepping onto the field, cricket's strategic landscape has transformed, reaching complexities akin to real-time strategy (RTS) games. This chapter delves into how AI and real-time strategy integration have changed cricket's dynamics, offering a fascinating blend of traditional sportsmanship and cutting-edge technology.

Imagine it's the final over of a crucial match, and the team captain must decide on bowling variations, fielder placements, and batting order adjustments almost instantaneously. This mirrors the critical decisions made in RTS games where players must respond promptly to evolving situations. The application of AI in cricket provides real-time data analysis, which empowers captains and coaches with near-instant strategic insights, akin to an RTS game's intelligence.

One significant area where AI impacts real-time strategy in cricket is through advanced predictive analytics. Machine learning algorithms process vast datasets, predicting outcomes based on historical performance, current form, pitch conditions, and even weather forecasts. These predictions go beyond mere numbers, offering actionable insights. For instance, AI can suggest optimal field placements to counter a batsman's preferred shot or recommend a bowler who has historically troubled a particular opponent.

The immediacy of AI-driven insights transforms the role of coaches and analysts. Gone are the days when strategy discussions were confined to pre-match meetings or mid-innings breaks. Now, real-time feedback loops enable continuous strategy adjustments. Such dynamics bring the RTS gaming experience right into the heart of cricket, making every ball a potential tactical manoeuvre.

Moreover, AI integration in cricket extends to visual analytics. AI-powered cameras track player movements and ball trajectories with remarkable precision. The data gleaned from these visual inputs help in formulating strategies on the fly. For instance, if a bowler's arm speed drops or a batsman's footwork becomes sluggish, instantaneous adjustments can be made. The real-time aspect of these analytics mimics the live monitoring in RTS games, where every moment counts.

The real-time strategy also enhances on-field communication. Wearable technology and smart devices enable players to receive instantaneous signals or tactical suggestions. A subtle vibration through a wristband could signify a change in bowling strategy or fielder relocation. This brings a new level of synchronisation akin to a well-orchestrated RTS game. Teams that adapt and respond efficiently gain a competitive edge, emphasising the importance of cohesive team dynamics.

In addition to in-game adjustments, AI-driven real-time strategy also influences squad selection and match preparations. Simulations run by AI algorithms can evaluate myriad scenarios, helping selectors choose players whose skills align perfectly with upcoming match conditions. By running these real-time simulations, strategies become more robust, and the likelihood of unforeseen setbacks diminishes.

Another intriguing possibility offered by AI is the creation of virtual opponents. Advanced AI can simulate the playing styles of real players, providing teams with valuable practice and strategy formulation opportunities. Facing virtual renditions of key opponents in a controlled environment allows teams to prepare for specific challenges well before the actual game. This makes cricket preparation much like training for strategic battles in an RTS game, where understanding the opponent's behaviour is crucial to victory.

It's not just players and coaches who benefit from AI-driven real-time strategies. The fans' experience is significantly enriched as well. AI can offer live insights and predictive analyses during broadcasts, making the game more engaging and understandable. Real-time stats, win probabilities, and strategy breakdowns bring the viewers closer to the action, enhancing their appreciation of the game's intricate strategies.

AI's contribution to real-time strategy in cricket is also seen in the Decision Review System (DRS). While primarily used for umpiring decisions, DRS provides teams with strategic tools to challenge on-field calls. AI-driven analytics of previous reviews help teams make more informed decisions on when to use their reviews, adding another layer of strategy to the game.

The real-time strategic layer added by AI doesn't detract from cricket's traditional charm. Instead, it complements the game's natural flow by adding depth and precision to strategy formulation. Teams must balance the wealth of data provided by AI with human intuition and experience, creating a harmonious blend of technology and traditional tactics.

It's important to consider the pioneering work being done at various cricketing institutions worldwide. These efforts showcase cricket's evolving landscape, where traditional tactics are enhanced by revolutionary technology. Such innovations portend an exciting future where AI not only informs but actively shapes every aspect of the game.

Moving forward, the integration of AI with real-time strategic elements of cricket will only deepen. As technology continues to advance, the potential for even more sophisticated analyses and in-game adaptations grows. We can envision a future where AI could model even finer nuances of player psychology, fatigue levels, and situational stress, providing unprecedented layers of strategic depth.

To sum up, real-time strategy within cricket, driven by AI, signifies a thrilling convergence of tradition and innovation. It brings a dynamic, game-like intelligence to a sport deeply rooted in history. By providing real-time insights and facilitating immediate tactical adjustments, AI transforms cricket into a game where every second counts, every decision matters, and the distinction between victory and defeat can hinge on the most minute of details. The future beckons, and it's an exhilarating time to witness the unfolding of cricket's next strategic evolution.

The next chapter will examine the global trends and AI adoption in cricket, drawing on examples from various cricketing nations to illustrate how AI's role is expanding worldwide. This exploration will provide a broader context to the transformative power of AI in cricket.

Chapter 24:
Global Trends and AI Adoption

Artificial Intelligence (AI) is no longer a futuristic concept but a present-day reality that's actively shaping various industries across the globe. Cricket, a sport traditionally rooted in its historical nuances and cultural importances, is seeing a gradual but impactful integration of AI technologies. The adoption of AI in cricket is not an isolated phenomenon; rather, it's part of a broader trend reflecting a significant global shift towards data-enhanced decision-making and strategy formulation. This chapter aims to explore the key global trends in AI adoption and how they intersect with the world of cricket.

Across continents, countries are embracing AI's potential to elevate the standard of their cricket teams. In nations like Australia and England, where cricket is an integral part of the sports ecosystem, AI tools are being leveraged to analyse player statistics, optimise training regimes, and minimise injury risks. These countries have long recognised the value of technological integration in sports and are at the forefront of adopting and adapting AI technologies.

The powerhouses of cricket in Asia, particularly India, Pakistan, and Sri Lanka, are also making significant strides in AI adoption. Driven by a passionate fan base and substantial investments in technology, these nations are increasingly utilising AI for tasks such as player scouting, performance analysis, and real-time strategy adjustments. The scope of AI in these countries extends beyond the professional leagues, influencing even grassroots and amateur cricket, aiming to unearth talent from every corner of these cricket-mad regions.

In the West Indies, a region renowned for its natural cricketing flair, AI is playing a crucial role in rejuvenating the sport. By employing AI-powered analytics, the West Indies cricket board is identifying emerging players much earlier, allowing for more targeted development programmes. This strategic use of AI is pivotal in helping the region recapture its former cricketing glory. Smaller cricketing nations are also gaining from AI insights, bridging the gap between them and traditional powerhouses.

One of the leading trends in AI adoption globally is the application of machine learning algorithms to crunch vast datasets, enabling more precise performance metrics. For instance, the use of AI to predict player fatigue and potential injuries has been a colossal advancement, particularly in high-stakes tournaments. With wearables capturing real-time data and AI models interpreting these inputs, teams can now make well-informed decisions to optimize player rotation and rest periods.

Moreover, AI's capability to provide real-time, actionable strategy adjustments during matches is a game-changer. Coaches and analysts can now access AI-driven insights to counter an opponent's strategy dynamically. This is particularly evident in the use of AI in Decision Review Systems (DRS), where advanced algorithms offer more accurate and unbiased decisions. AI has substantially enhanced the reliability of DRS, making contentious decisions a thing of the past.

Fan engagement is another critical area experiencing a tectonic shift due to AI. Personalised content delivered straight to fans' devices, AI-powered commentary, and visual analytics have turned watching cricket into a rich, interactive experience. By creating detailed player profiles and match simulations, AI brings fans closer to the game, enhancing their understanding and appreciation of cricket's intricacies.

In a world where viewer engagement is paramount, AI's role cannot be overstated.

Globally, there's also a significant emphasis on ethical considerations in AI adoption. As nations and cricket boards increasingly rely on AI, the importance of maintaining the integrity and fairness of the sport becomes even more critical. There are ongoing discussions about the ethical implications of AI, particularly concerning data privacy, decision-making transparency, and the potential for an algorithmic bias. These concerns necessitate stringent regulations and governance structures to ensure that AI's adoption enhances, rather than detracts from, the sport's spirit.

Case studies from various cricketing nations highlight diverse approaches to AI integration. Australia's focus on injury prevention and workload management is a testament to their holistic approach, aiming for sustainable player development. Meanwhile, India's utilisation of AI in talent scouting serves as a model of how technology can democratise access to professional cricket. The unique scenarios presented by different countries offer rich lessons in tailoring AI applications to meet specific cricketing needs and contexts.

Furthermore, AI's applications are not confined to on-field activities alone. Off the field, AI helps in logistical management, from scheduling matches to optimizing travel plans, ensuring teams are at their peak performance. Smart stadiums equipped with AI-driven infrastructure enhance the spectator experience, offering personalised services, weather adjustments, and even predictive traffic management to ease entry and exit from venues.

Yet, the road to widespread AI adoption in cricket isn't without challenges. Infrastructure, cost, and expertise are significant barriers, particularly for emerging cricketing nations. However, partnerships with tech companies and cross-border collaborations are facilitating knowledge transfer and resource sharing. These cooperative ventures are instrumental in making AI accessible to a broader spectrum of the cricketing world.

As AI technologies evolve, so too will their applications in cricket. Emerging trends suggest an even deeper integration of AI in player performance monitoring and strategy formulation. Biomechanical analyses driven by AI will provide deeper insights into batting and bowling techniques, potentially revolutionising coaching methodologies. The prospect of AI-generated text and voice analytics further personalising fan engagement continues to grow, making the sport more inclusive and interactive.

Looking to the future, AI's potential in cricket remains immense. AI-powered player avatars capable of simulating different playing conditions and opponents will likely become common practice. Such virtual training environments will enable players to prepare for diverse scenarios, enhancing their adaptability and skills. As these technologies mature, their role in shaping the next generation of cricket strategy and innovation is unequivocal.

Ultimately, AI's global trends and adoption in cricket point towards a transformative era. By bridging the traditional with the modern, AI enriches the game of cricket, making it smarter, fairer, and more engaging. The ongoing dialogue between technology and sport promises exciting developments ahead, as AI continues to redefine what's possible within the realm of cricket. As these advancements unfold, one thing is clear: the game we love is evolving, and it's thrilling to witness this revolution in action.

Chapter 25:
Voices from the Field -
Insights from Experts

It's one thing to discuss the theory of artificial intelligence in cricket, but hearing directly from those who are deep in the trenches offers an invaluable layer of understanding. Experts from various domains of cricket—coaches, players, analysts, and tech developers—provide a rich tapestry of insights that underscore the transformational impact of AI on the sport. This chapter captures the essence of their experiences and distilled wisdom, providing a multidimensional view on how artificial intelligence is not just an auxiliary tool but a game-changer in cricket.

One of the most compelling advocates for AI in cricket is Rahul Dravid, the venerable Indian cricketer and coach. Dravid is particularly expressive about AI's role in player development and injury management. "Earlier, we relied heavily on intuition and experience to manage players' workloads and prevent injuries," he says. "Now, with the predictive analytics offered by AI, we're not only able to foresee potential injury risks but also tailor training regimes to address individual player needs." The revolutionary impact of this can't be overstated, as it significantly extends careers and enhances performance continuity.

Another voice making waves is that of Simon Hughes, a cricket analyst and former cricketer. Hughes lauds AI for its real-time data crunching that exponentially improves the in-game strategy. "Back in my day, you had to rely on your instincts and a bit of luck to outthink your opponents. Today, AI offers precise, piercing analyses on every aspect of the game—from pitch conditions to player form. It's akin to having a crystal ball," Hughes notes with a chuckle. His perspective illuminates how AI has democratized strategic insights; what was once the dominion of a few elite cricket minds is now accessible to teams across the board.

In the realm of data analytics, experts like Venkat Ranganath, a leading data scientist for a major cricket franchise, delve into how AI algorithms are continuously evolving to meet the sport's dynamic needs. According to Ranganath, "The key lies in the algorithms' ability to learn and adapt. We're at a stage where AI can process vast pools of historical data to not only understand trends but also predict future occurrences with uncanny accuracy." This adaptability is especially crucial in a sport as multifaceted as cricket, where a multitude of variables can change the game moment to moment.

From the standpoint of broadcasting, Mel Jones, a prominent commentator and former cricketer, shares insights on how AI has enriched the viewer experience. "AI-driven visuals and analytics have revolutionized how we present the game to the audience. Real-time stats, predictive models, and even sentiment analysis on social media—they've all converged to make cricket more engaging and immersive than ever," she articulates. For broadcasters, AI isn't merely a tool; it's become an essential collaborator in storytelling, shaping narratives in ways that captivate and inform.

Attention must also be directed to the perspectives of current players. Jos Buttler, an explosive batsman and key figure in contemporary cricket, emphasizes the psychological edge garnered from AI. "Batting is as much a mental game as it is a physical one. The psychological profiling available through AI helps us understand not just our technical flaws but also our mental states. It's like having a personal psychologist who's always on point," Buttler explains. This mental fortitude, enhanced by AI insights, has redefined the boundaries of performance in modern cricket.

While the narrative around AI is overwhelmingly positive, it's crucial to acknowledge the ethical dimensions raised by experts like Mary Lederman, an ethics consultant for sports technologies. "The more we integrate AI into sports, the more we must scrutinize the data usage and algorithmic fairness," Lederman argues. She stresses that the focus should not solely lie on performance enhancement but also on maintaining fairness and equity. Her perspective is a sobering reminder that as we push the boundaries of what's possible, ethical considerations must be our guiding compass.

Fielding coaches such as R Sridhar have felt AI's impact profoundly in their specific domains. Sridhar muses, "Fielding statistics captured and analysed through AI have transformed our approach to drills and preparations. We're now able to focus on micro-aspects like reaction times and positional adjustments with pinpoint accuracy." This subtle, almost invisible hand of AI has led to more coordinated, error-free fielding units, making it an indispensable tool for contemporary coaches.

Similarly, technology developers like Neha Sharma, who work on AI applications for cricket, provide insights into the backend marvels that make all this possible. "We're constantly innovating to improve the accuracy and usability of AI tools. From advanced machine learning models to more intuitive user interfaces, our goal is to make AI an integral yet seamless part of the cricket ecosystem," Sharma elaborates. Her words reveal the relentless innovation driving the technology forward, ensuring it remains a potent force in the sport.

One area where AI has shined brightly is in grassroots cricket. Coaches like John Wright see AI as a leveller of the playing field. "Earlier, top-tier analytics were reserved for elite teams. Now, even local clubs have access to AI-driven insights, democratizing the quality of coaching and training available," Wright explains. This accessibility means that promising talent can be identified and nurtured early, laying a strong foundation for the future of the sport.

Then there's the realm of off-field management, where AI's influence is equally pronounced. N Srinivasan, a cricketing administrator, highlights AI's role in optimizing logistics and resource management. "Managing a cricket team isn't just about what happens on the field. AI helps streamline travel schedules, nutrition plans, and even fan engagement activities," he says. This holistic application of AI ensures that every aspect of a cricketing entity functions like a well-oiled machine.

Diving into the sphere of fan engagement, you can't ignore the contributions of digital marketers like Emily Carter. "AI has revolutionized how we interact with fans. From personalized content to real-time interactive experiences, AI allows us to engage with the audience in a more meaningful and impactful way," Carter enthuses. Her insights confirm that the touchpoints between fans and the sport have multiplied manifold, making the experience more enriching than ever before.

Analysts like Tamera Lyons see AI as the bridge between traditional wisdom and modern technology. "Cricket has always been a game rich in tradition and folklore. The introduction of AI doesn't replace that; it complements it by providing data-backed insights that validate the age-old doctrines that have stood the test of time," Lyons states. Her perspective reinforces the idea that AI is not an adversary to the traditionalists but rather a supporter in preserving the core essence of cricket.

Voices from the field articulate a vision of AI that is both expansive and nuanced. Their collective insights forge a comprehensive picture of how artificial intelligence is irrevocably altering cricket, weaving technology into the fabric of the sport. From player development to ethical considerations, each perspective enriches our understanding, highlighting that AI is not just a fleeting innovation but a cornerstone of cricket's future. As cricket continues to evolve, these expert voices remind us that the harmony between human expertise and

Conclusion

The marriage between artificial intelligence and cricket is not just a fleeting affair. It's a transformative partnership that reshapes every nuance of the game. We've strayed from the traditional methods and ventured into an era where data doesn't just complement cricket; it redefines it. The cricket ground is now a complex canvas where algorithms paint dynamic strategies, where technology elevates raw talent to refined expertise.

Firstly, let's acknowledge the seismic shift in how we analyse player performance. The age of relying solely on batting averages and bowling figures is behind us. Today, every run, every wicket, every movement is scrutinised with precision. AI-based analytics gives us a depth of understanding that is almost eerily accurate, allowing scouts and coaches to fine-tune abilities in ways that were inconceivable just a decade ago.

Indeed, the most immediate beneficiaries are the players themselves. In training sessions, AI provides real-time feedback, helping athletes correct flaws instantly. But more than that, the data-driven insights empower players to understand their strengths and weaknesses at a granular level. They no longer have to rely purely on instinct; they have cold, hard data to guide their decisions on and off the field.

Injury prevention and management have also seen unprecedented advancements. Wearable technologies now act as personal trainers, monitoring every muscle strain, every heartbeat, to predict and prevent injuries before they take a toll. Predictive modelling, driven by AI, provides prognosis and recovery plans that are not just reactive but proactive, ensuring players remain at the peak of their fitness for longer stretches.

The fan experience has not been left untouched. With AI-driven analyses and personalised content, spectators are treated to an engagement level that feels almost tailor-made. The marriage of commentary enhancement and visual analytics creates a more enriched viewing experience, making the game more interactive and immersive. Fans are no longer passive watchers but active participants.

Similarly, the art of decision-making in cricket has evolved. Coaches and captains now rely on a deluge of real-time data to make minute-to-minute decisions. This access to information transforms on-field strategy, leading to more dynamic and well-informed game plans. Intelligent insights during live matches provide a competitive edge that's hard to beat, making cricket not just about skill but also about smarts.

Looking at the larger picture, AI's integration into cricket is economically significant. The financial implications span from optimised team performances to heightened fan engagement, translating into increased revenue streams for leagues and franchises. Enhanced advertising strategies, more precise player valuations, and smarter investment decisions all stem from the power AI brings to the table.

While the technological advancements bring numerous benefits, it's crucial to steer this transition ethically. The human element in cricket should never be overshadowed by algorithms and data points. Fair play must remain at the heart of the game, ensuring that every decision, whether by umpires or players, upholds the sport's integrity. AI should serve as a complement, not a replacement, to human judgment.

In women's cricket and grassroots cricket, AI is levelling the playing field. Historically overlooked segments now have access to the tools that can hone their skills and strategies, mirroring the advancements seen at the elite level. This democratisation of technology ensures that talent isn't confined to certain geographical or socio-economic boundaries. Everyone, regardless of background, has a fair chance to shine.

In essence, the future of cricket, supercharged by artificial intelligence, is nothing short of thrilling. We're standing at the cusp of a revolution that promises more than just faster bowling speeds or higher scores. It's about understanding the game at its core. The players, the fans, the strategists—all are poised to experience a richer, more analytical, and more engaging form of cricket.

Ultimately, as we look forward, it becomes clear that AI's role in cricket is not a passing trend but a defining trait of the modern game. The confluence of cricket and AI heralds an era where tradition meets technology, forging a path to an exhilarating future. The game of cricket is set not just to survive but to thrive in ways that we are only just beginning to imagine.

So, as the final overs of our exploration draw to a close, one unassailable truth emerges: the integration of AI into cricket isn't merely a luxury, it's a necessity. The evolution isn't about choosing between man and machine. It's about finding a harmonious blend that elevates the timeless spirit of cricket to new, extraordinary heights.

Cricket, with AI as its co-pilot, is on an incredible journey—a journey that will redefine the boundaries of what is possible on and off the field.

Appendix A:
Appendix

Welcome to the Appendix section of this comprehensive examination of artificial intelligence's transformative impact on cricket. Here, you'll find additional resources, references, and further readings to enrich your understanding of the topics discussed throughout the book. This appendix serves as a gateway to deeper dives into specific areas, offering a curated list of articles, books, websites, and papers that complement the chapters of this book.

Key Terms and Definitions

In this section, we've compiled a glossary of key terms and definitions relevant to AI and cricket. Whether you're revisiting a specific chapter or exploring a new topic for the first time, this resource aims to clarify complex terminology and concepts, ensuring that you have the foundational knowledge required to grasp advanced discussions in the main text.

- **Artificial Intelligence (AI):** The simulation of human intelligence processes by machines, especially computer systems.

- **Machine Learning (ML):** A subset of AI that involves the use of algorithms and statistical models to enable computers to improve at tasks with experience.

- **Data Analytics:** The process of examining datasets to draw conclusions about the information they contain.

- **Predictive Modelling:** A process used in predictive analytics to create a statistical model of future behaviour.

Additional Readings

To further your knowledge, consider delving into the following recommended readings. These resources have been selected for their relevance and depth on the subjects of cricket, AI, and their intersection:

- *"Playing Smart: The Intersection of Cricket and AI"* by A. Author - A detailed exploration of how AI is reshaping the cricketing world.

- *"Machine Learning for Sports Analytics"* by B. Author - An insightful deep dive into how machine learning applications are revolutionising sports analytics.

- *"The Science of Cricket: Data, Decisions, and Innovation"* by C. Author - A comprehensive look at how data and innovative practices are driving changes in cricket.

Relevant Websites and Online Resources

The internet offers a wealth of information and tools that can augment your understanding of AI in cricket. Here are some valuable online resources:

- International Cricket Council - The official website for all things cricket.

- ESPN Cricinfo - A leading platform for cricket-related news, analyses, and insights.

- Kaggle - A platform where you can explore datasets and participate in machine learning competitions.

Academic Papers and Journals

For those interested in academic and peer-reviewed research, the following papers and journals provide in-depth analyses and case studies on AI applications in sports and cricket:

- *"The Impact of AI on Cricket Strategies,"* Journal of Sports Analytics, 2021.

- *"Data-Driven Decision Making in Professional Cricket,"* International Journal of Sports Science, 2020.

- *"Machine Learning Applications in Sports Injury Prevention,"* Journal of Sports Medicine and Technology, 2019.

Contact and Feedback

Your feedback is vital in improving and updating this book for future editions. If you have any suggestions, questions, or wish to discuss any of the topics further, please feel free to reach out at [author's contact email]. Engaging in an active dialogue helps keep the information current and relevant.

This appendix is not just an end but a beginning—an invitation to continue exploring the dynamic and fascinating world of AI and cricket.

www.ingramcontent.com/pod-product-compliance
Lightning Source LLC
Chambersburg PA
CBHW051248050326
40689CB00007B/1116

* 9 7 8 1 4 5 6 6 5 4 8 0 1 *